FAITH IN THE FIRE

ALSO BY GARDNER C. TAYLOR

Books

The Words of Gardner Taylor, Volume 1:
The NBC Radio Sermons, 1959–1970

The Words of Gardner Taylor, Volume 2:
Sermons from the Middle Years, 1970–1980

The Words of Gardner Taylor, Volume 3:
Quintessential Classics, 1980–Present

The Words of Gardner Taylor, Volume 4:
Special Occasion and Expository Sermons

The Words of Gardner Taylor, Volume 5:
Lectures, Essays, and Interviews

The Words of Gardner Taylor, Volume 6:
50 Years of Timeless Treasures

Gardner Taylor 90th Birthday Collection

Perfecting the Pastor's Art (with G. Avery Taylor)

We Have the Ministry: The Heart of the Pastor's Vocation (with Dr. Samuel Proctor)

DVDs/CDs/Cassettes

The Words of Gardner Taylor Preaching Library on CD-ROM

Essential Taylor Audiocassette

Essential Taylor CD

Essential Taylor II Audiocassette

Essential Taylor II CD

Please visit: Hay House USA: **www.hayhouse.com**®;
Hay House Australia: **www.hayhouse.com.au**;
Hay House UK: **www.hayhouse.co.uk**; Hay House South Africa:
www.hayhouse.co.za; Hay House India: **www.hayhouse.co.in**

FAITH IN THE FIRE
Wisdom for Life

GARDNER C. TAYLOR

Edited by Edward L. Taylor

SMILEYBOOKS

Distributed by Hay House, Inc.
Carlsbad, California • New York City
London • Sydney • Johannesburg
Vancouver • Hong Kong • New Delhi

Copyright © 2011 by Gardner C. Taylor
Introduction © Copyright 2011 Edward L. Taylor

Published in the United States by: SmileyBooks, 250 Park Avenue South, Suite #201, New York, NY 10003 • www.SmileyBooks.com

Distributed in the United States by: Hay House, Inc.: www.hayhouse.com • ***Published and distributed in Australia by:*** Hay House Australia Pty. Ltd.: www.hayhouse.com.au • ***Published and distributed in the United Kingdom by:*** Hay House UK, Ltd.: www.hayhouse.co.uk • ***Published and distributed in the Republic of South Africa by:*** Hay House SA (Pty), Ltd.: www.hayhouse.co.za • ***Distributed in Canada by:*** Raincoast: www.raincoast.com • ***Published and distributed in India by:*** Hay House Publishers India: www.hayhouse.co.in

Interior design: Julie Davison
Interior photos: Credits in text

All rights reserved. No part of this book may be reproduced by any mechanical, photographic, or electronic process, or in the form of a phonographic recording; nor may it be stored in a retrieval system, transmitted, or otherwise be copied for public or private use—other than for "fair use" as brief quotations embodied in articles and reviews—without prior written permission of the publisher.

The opinions set forth herein are those of the author, and do not necessarily express the views of the publisher or Hay House, Inc., or any of its affiliates.

Library of Congress Control Number: 2011925372

Hardcover ISBN: 978-1-4019-2962-6
Digital ISBN: 978-1-4019-2963-3

14 13 12 11   4 3 2 1
1st edition, August 2011

Printed in the United States of America

*To the Progressive National Baptist Convention
on the occasion of your 50th Anniversary.*

*For your bright shining progressive witness
of fellowship, service, and peace*

1961–2011

CONTENTS

Introduction xi

Chapter 1: On God 1
Chapter 2: A God Worth Serving 17
Chapter 3: The Way of Love 29
Chapter 4: Culture and Politics 39
Chapter 5: Embracing Hope 63
Chapter 6: The Basis of a Christian's Courage 73
Chapter 7: Have Patience 83
Chapter 8: The Matter of Race 93
Chapter 9: It's All in the Family 107
Chapter 10: Everyday Wit 121
Chapter 11: Laughter Is Good for the Soul 145
Chapter 12: Life's Journey 169
Chapter 13: The Sweetening of Life 187
Chapter 14: Faith in the Fire 199

Appendices

My Favorite Things 212
Acknowledgments 215
About the Author 216
About the Editor 217

INTRODUCTION

The legendary giant Gardner Calvin Taylor has intrigued and fascinated me for decades. I first learned about him in the late 1980s. During a chance meeting at a local drugstore in my hometown of Ville Platte, Louisiana, my pastor, M. L. Thomas, and I started chatting about the annual session of the National Baptist Convention of America. Responding to my query about the high moments of the convention, Pastor Thomas immediately replied that Gardner Taylor was a guest preacher and he was "unbelievable." He unconsciously shook his head left to right several times like a person who had witnessed something amazing, but could not believe that which he saw. The name Gardner Taylor did not escape me. Audiotapes of his preaching occasionally came into my possession. Later, I learned of a weekly Baton Rouge radio broadcast hosted by his friend Carl Stewart that featured many of his messages. Sunday after Sunday, I listened to this Baton Rouge preacher borrowed by Brooklyn who wove a seamless, sermonic tapestry unlike anything I had ever heard.

A native of Baton Rouge, Louisiana, Gardner Taylor was born in 1918 to Reverend Washington Monroe Taylor and Salina Taylor. After receiving his education in Baton Rouge's segregated public schools, he went on to earn degrees from Leland College in 1937 and Oberlin Graduate School of Theology in 1940, as well as 15 honorary doctorates. After serving pastorates in Elyria, Ohio, and New Orleans, Louisiana, Gardner Taylor was called to First African Mount Zion Baptist Church in Baton Rouge, Louisiana, the pulpit once occupied by his father. In 1948, Taylor became pastor of the Concord Baptist Church of Brooklyn, New York, the church where he earned his reputation as a champion fighter for social justice and community uplift, and received acclaim as one of the greatest preachers in American history. Moreover, his hands-on experiences as a negotiator for equal pay for Louisiana's African American teachers, as New York City's second African American school board member, and co-leader in the triumvirate that led Brooklyn's Democratic Party, all shaped and reinforced his belief in radical engagement to agitate for racial inclusion and community improvement. Indeed, Taylor, using his powerful voice as the bullhorn for change, called for public action by people who care about their society and democratic values.

During his pastorate in New York City, Taylor amassed an enviable record of noteworthy accomplishments. Concord Church established a nursing home, an elementary school, a federal credit union, a clothing exchange, multiple units of low-income housing, and a million-dollar Christ Fund for youth and community development. In 1952, when Concord was ravaged by fire, he successfully led his congregation through a difficult reconstruction effort at a cost of more than $1.8 million.

If these achievements had been the only accomplishments of Gardner Taylor, his record would be regarded with respect and his reputation as a minister would be renowned around the world. However, Gardner Taylor's contribution to the call and art of preaching is what has brought him his greatest fame. From early in his ministry until the present day, he has been cited as a prince of the Protestant pulpit. In 1956, *Ebony* magazine named him one of America's Bright Young Men of God. In 1979, *Time* magazine named him one of the seven greatest preachers of the American Protestant pulpit. *Ebony,* again, recognized Taylor's oratorical gifts by naming him one of the 15 greatest preachers in America in 1984 and 1993. *Newsweek* magazine cited Baylor University's 1993 recognition of Dr. Taylor as one of the 12 greatest preachers in the English-speaking world.

President William Jefferson Clinton awarded Gardner Taylor the Presidential Medal of Freedom in 2000 as an acknowledgment of his public service as New York City's second African American school board member; of the impact he had as the first African American to head a political party in one of the boroughs of New York City; and for his outstanding contributions to religious life as a preacher.

I finally met Dr. Taylor while studying at Louisiana College in March of 1992 during a series of preaching engagements he fulfilled in Alexandria, Louisiana. The powerful imagery of his language, cogent arguments, and homiletical genius arrested my attention. We have since developed a unique bond that has played an unbelievably large and important role in my life. Although we are not related, we are soil-kin, both reared in the bosom of Louisiana (though decades apart), a fact that binds us as well as many other Bayou State preachers into an informal family with deep roots in rich traditions. *The Words of Gardner Taylor,* a multivolume compilation of Dr. Taylor's orations and writings, has

Introduction

been the most widely publicized outcome of our work together thus far. It has been my pleasure to serve as the editor of Dr. Taylor's latest work.

Faith in the Fire: Wisdom for Life adds a unique contribution to Dr. Taylor's legacy by attempting to gather his philosophical gems and present them in a fashion that readers can easily access. The collection begins with "On God." Dr. Taylor–ever the faithful Christian and tireless preacher–has voiced innumerable passages that reflect his belief and confidence in an eternal being, and illustrate how God is ever-present, guiding, powerful, and loving.

Delivered in the Concord pulpit, "A God Worth Serving" is the first of three sermons included in this work. Gardner Taylor's message urges those who believe to enter into a relationship with the Eternal because God is "above and yet close." In Dr. Taylor's opinion, the nature of God beckons us to service in God's name and for the profit of God's Kingdom.

"The Way of Love" is a testament to Dr. Taylor's belief that love is an outgrowth of our relationship with the One who is greater than us. Therefore, we accept, care, and honor each other and ourselves in the spirit of love. For Dr. Taylor, love is the fundamental element by which we should live—an adhesive that binds us together and inspires our efforts toward a better world.

"Culture and Politics" is a reflection on the state of American life. There lies in Dr. Taylor a belief deeply entrenched in commitment to politics because social justice and equality may be secured through government. His political views were formed in the crucible of the segregated South and from his discovery of differing sensibilities on race during his residence in Ohio and New York City. Because of these experiences, Gardner Taylor developed a philosophy of culture and politics—the practice of engagement. This means all persons should commit to being active partcipants in their community and government.

"Embracing Hope" and "Have Patience" highlight some of Dr. Taylor's comments on what he believes are critical characteristics of successful people. He believes the culture of nihilism dissipates when confronted by hope. Dr. Taylor understands hope as an expression of soul in the midst of circumstances beyond our control, and believes that present conditions of discouragement are temporary situations awaiting a brighter and better future. This is to say, patience is understood as the capacity to await hope's fulfillment. These elements distinguish those who reach the pinnacle of great achievement from those who don't even try.

"The Basis of a Christian's Courage," his second message from Concord, speaks of courage as a trait easily discussed, but difficult to exhibit. All who travel life's journey are certain to encounter crises, challenges, and critical circumstances. Gardner Taylor suggests that people of faith have within them a deep spiritual reservoir from which to draw a firmness of faith that allows them to face the fiercest foes of life bravely. Such bravery of spirit is courage.

"The Matter of Race" may be the most defining aspect of Gardner Taylor's life. His efforts toward racial equality, especially those during the civil rights movement, have permeated his entire adult life. Those who are not privileged to have lived through the civil rights movement cannot fully appreciate this revolution's impact on America's culture of race. Indeed, the history of race relations and attempts at its improvement continues to occupy significant space in the social conversation and cultural life of the United States. Heavily influenced by his personal experiences, Dr. Taylor participated in this national discussion through private conversations with presidents, chats and arguments with his long-time friend Dr. Martin Luther King, Jr., and public discourse from the Concord pulpit and other platforms around the world. "Race" explores core cultural beliefs, social and civil equality of races, and how they are interwoven with humanity's destiny.

"It's All in the Family" makes a case for strengthening society's primary institution and ensuring its survival. To be sure, Gardner Taylor was shaped by the nobility and respect found in Louisiana's southern culture. His formative years belonged to an era in which young men were taught a certain sense of respectability, composure, and dignity that was to be observed by gentlemen. Dr. Taylor summons the nation to those fundamental values he believes are inherent in family life. His writings describe his dream for a society that acknowledges parental responsibilities to their young and children's respectful attitudes toward parents.

"Everyday Wit" and "Laughter Is Good for the Soul" provide interesting insight into Gardner Taylor's personality. As one reads these pages, a certain delightful sense of his warmth and sense of humor shine through. Yet, that sense cannot compare with being in his presence, hearing his voice as he communicates deep truths, weaves enabling stories, formulates arguments, and engenders hilarious and uncontrollable laughter. These sections paint a portrait of the profundity of the great orator's individuality, character, and charm on the canvas of his humanity. Experiencing these traits will leave readers with rewarding joy.

"Life's Journey" contains cherished insights collected from years of experience seasoned with joys and heartaches from his journey. He bore his father's death at the impressionable age of 12, Concord Church's destruction

Introduction

by fire, and the heartbreaking loss of his first wife, Laura, to a tragic pedestrian accident. Conversely, Gardner Taylor has experienced many triumphs, such as taking the helm of Concord's reconstruction of its million-dollar church edifice, an attempt that, at the time, had not been accomplished by any urban African American congregation. He delivered the 100th Lyman Beecher Lectures at Yale University, addressed the Baptist World Alliance five times, and delivered the sermon during the inaugural worship service for President William Clinton. Through those profound experiences Dr. Taylor helps us to understand that life's journey is a blessed combination of blisses and burdens.

"The Sweetening of Life," the third sermon included in this book, is a message about faith as an enabling force for those who must face the fact that life draws to an end. Faith in something greater than us—faith in God—makes each day a little better even when we know not many remain. Bitter days are better days with the sweetness of faith. One cannot help but being greatly moved at the thought that these words were originally penned nearly 50 years ago, but are not seen through the eyes of one in his 90s.

Faith has been the scarlet thread that weaves the fabric of *Faith in the Fire* together. It is also the subject of the eponymous final chapter, which outlines

Dr. Taylor's vision of what is the most essential tool for our human odyssey. Gardner Taylor has determined that God inspires us to faith and that our faith in God, ourselves, and others does sustain us along treacherous paths of life. Real faith allows us to cope, endure, and persevere. This kind of faith is the faith that protects us in the fire of life's inevitable challenges.

After years of collecting and editing his writings for publication, I am privileged to have in my home nearly every sermon manuscript and set of recordings Dr. Taylor delivered at Concord Church between 1948 and 1990, as well as copies of most of his other writings, sermons, speeches, and other available sources. After months of mining these sermons and his latest proclamations by pen found in his recent forays into blogging in *On Faith* by the *Washington Post,* I selected the entries found in *Faith in the Fire.* Words cannot express the honor and joy that is mine for having been entrusted with so great a task as to compile and edit Dr. Gardner Taylor's life work.

Save for the three previously mentioned sermons, my selections are not sermons printed in whole. Nor are these writings meant to represent Dr. Taylor's final word on each subject. Rather, these are slices of prophetic reflections taken in part from his 70 years as a published writer, pulpit preacher, and public intellectual. However as sermons are a significant source for this book, it must be stated that sermons and other forms of public oration lose something when not heard. They become handcuffed and arrested, so to speak. In this case, thankfully, that which is lost to the ear does not rob the eye, mind, and heart of blessings. Those blessings are life lessons that instruct, inspire, and hearten. Although not rendered as sermons, his words do remind one of a nearly forgotten era pretelevision, when educated African American preachers first began to engage in cross-cultural religious life in a biblical, sensible, and cosmopolitan intellectual manner, standing flat-footed and boldly proclaiming a message of hope to all.

Though Dr. Gardner C. Taylor's writings, speeches, and sermons have been published in many forms, and have achieved remarkable fame and respect in religious circles, precious few of these treasures have found their way to the general reader. Amazingly, many people of faith and members of the reading public have not heard of Gardner Taylor or his accomplishments. Publication of *Faith in the Fire* attempts to rectify this by providing an accessible introduction to Dr. Taylor's enduring wisdom. My hope and prayer is that this treasured volume will bless all who seek *Faith in the Fire*.

Edward Taylor
London, England

CHAPTER ONE

ON GOD

Our God is as great as God is good and as good as God is great, and this is to say marvelous things about both God's goodness and God's greatness. The God we serve merits our reverence, bowed heads, bent knees, and trembling spirits, the touch of a whisper in our voices and unstudied pauses of silence when we talk with God. Our God is different from us creatures, but God is as God ever was, and was as God ever will be. I bow before God, because God is without start and without finish, is without increase and without decrease, never grows better because He is already, and ever was, perfect. God never grows worse because in God there is no changing. God demands and receives my unqualified reverence.

Love is a part of the character of God. By that love, we are blessed. We should not take for granted the love and blessings of God. There are so many people to whom God has been exceedingly good and abundantly kind. How marvelous this life is because God has opened a way for us—a way of good health, good fortune, and good circumstances. Because of this care, we should in turn offer our lives, time, loyalty, and our own love to God. We love God because God loved us first. Our God is love.

We know that God loves us. There was food on our table this morning, and light of God was in the sky when we awoke. Prophets have told us that God loves us. No matter how people look at it, never mind what explanations they give, we know that God was at work there, in our interest and at a great cost. Ask pilgrims midway through their journey home. Eavesdrop on the praise of the redeemed in the city of our God.

On God

Forgiveness is a part of the nature of God. Individuals and our nation can receive this forgiveness. In these trying and difficult days, all should bow to ask God for grace and humility, that forgiveness may be extended. God will not regard us with favor if we are forever flexing our muscles and proclaiming our richness and greatness. We need admit our failures and confess our faults and ask for understanding as we strive to make up our delinquencies. A glad God will forgive. Therefore, let us also forgive one another. Remember, an ugly look, a harsh word may pour salt into an already aching heart. On the other hand, a kind word may be a salve and balm to that poor, broken spirit. God will forgive as we forgive each other.

✢

God wants us to live one day at a time. We know there may be something waiting for us which we dread, shrink back from with an awful terror. Stop concentrating on it. God often does not grant us grace in advance, but I have found God faithful in giving grace, as we need it. Grace on a daily basis. God gives us daily strength, courage, hope, and power. I have not found God absent in the hour of need, nor God's mercy missing in the time of a cry.

It is the burden of the Gospel that we are not far off from God, aliens, or worse, orphans beneath a leaden sky. . . . We are listed as individual and precious assets on the ledgers of God. . . . A soul believing that his or her life is ordered of God is restored to a peace that the world can neither give nor take away. . . . There, God, once and for all, has assessed our value to His heart. . . . There is one huge, eternally valid act God has thrown in for us, and our salvation is what God's heart considers to be our worth to Him. . . . That great passage which begins "God so loved the world" is aimed not alone at humanity, but everything in the world.

✢

All people have some God in them. That is exactly what the Bible says. God purposed you in His heart so that you are not impromptu, something gotten up on the spur of the moment. Something in God ached for your creation and cried out that you and I, and those like us, would come to pass. In the counsels of God's reflection, behind history and before time, God spoke to Godself, the Bible suggests, and said, "Let us make man in Our image, after Our likeness. So God created man in His own image, in the image of God created He him."

On God

We are likely to feel we are so far removed from God that He finds it hard dealing with us, doesn't know how to mange us, can't understand us. There is in us some of God, no matter how far down we've pushed it, and how we've tried to hide it all behind the bed or to sweep it beneath the rug, so to speak. And God still knows about us, no matter how far we've wandered. Something is saying God loves you still.

There resides enough God in us so that what He had to say could reach us. He knew the stubborn depths of evil in us, and yet He knew that down beneath the dirt and grime, the crust of hard and great evil, there resided a basic image, the likeness of God. There was disappointment, yes because the God in us is so often submerged beneath so much else. "As many as received Him, to them He gave power to become the children of God." The likeness of God is still in us, still in our American society. The image of God may be marred in our society, but heaven be praised, it is carved deep in the thought and heart of America. There is God in you and me. So seeing and so setting ourselves, the presence of God becomes our desired climate, and we live our days in His sight as if all He bids us see and seek is the fullness of the stature of Christ.

God has a plan for your life if you are within covenant relationship with God. If you will not accept your part in the contractual relationship He proposes, then the contract is null and void, of no effect, nonbinding! On the other hand, if you are in covenant relationship, God has a plan for you . . . and all the devils in hell cannot defeat it. So do not linger in panic. The first thing a Christian ought to remember is the plan.

When trouble comes, remember the plan. God is not trapped. He is not baffled. He is not without resources. Remember that it takes winter to make springtime, and that God turns stumbling blocks into stepping-stones, and remember that God can turn midnight into daybreak. Never forget that God can make a way when there is no way, bring peace out of confusion, pick up the downtrodden, feed the hungry, and help the helpless.

✢

God, to be our God, must enter the arena of our troubles, the theater of our operation. This is at the heart of the good news we call the Gospel: We have a God who comes where we are. We can hear in the distance the cry of one who has stood over a fallen and wounded race and has watched the God of all the earth feel their loneliness, participate in their heartbreak. We have no less a Gospel than that God is kin to us. One hears the words of the brave old Book and takes hope, for our hearts wait for a God who can feel our sorrow and share our heart's desires.

---

*Even God troubles us, annoys, and antagonizes us,
by telling intelligent, supposedly well-adjusted,
respectable people that they are lost without God.
God says to us in so many places and in so many ways
that we cannot deal with Him until we humble ourselves. . . .
God will guide us, but only when humbly we confess,
"I cannot find my way and I am far from home." God will
strengthen us, but only when humbly we confess, "I am weak,
but Thou art mighty." God will feed us, with heavenly food,
but only when we humbly plead, "Bread of Heaven,
Bread of Heaven, feed me till I want no more."
God confronts us all with our pride and our high-mindedness.*

We have enough God. Enough God is a god who can get low enough to reach you and me and to understand who we are, what we are, and where we are. We cannot use a god who cannot get close enough to us to be able to take our pulse and understand what our condition is. It may be a wonderful and grand deity, but there is no practical value to me if my god cannot understand where I am and what I am. If my god can understand what I am and who I am and where I am and cannot do anything about it, I don't have enough God. What we have to have is a God with power and with tenderness, a God most wonderfully kind, and a God almighty. If my god doesn't understand my tears and my heartbreak, my grief, my longings, my aspirations, it is very little, no matter how powerful he might be, that he can do for me. If a god understands my thoughts afar off and he knows my down-sitting and my uprising and he can't do anything about it, he's not enough God for me. Our God is enough God.

✢

Almost all of us have come to some hard and nigh-impossible hour, and we have called upon God and asked God to please deliver us. . . . God would be our God and we would be God's children. That is the place of God, where

God was real in our lives, where God spoke peace to our troubled spirits, where God claimed us for His own.

Sometimes it seems as if things are never going to work out. It appears that we will never have peace because we have wandered so far from God, that God does not seem real in our lives. We need to go back to the place where God spoke to us. I know we cannot go back physically to those places and scenes where God spoke to us. But, we can recall the house where we learned of God, or go back in the Spirit and start over where we left God. We can thank God that when trouble is on our trial, we can say to it, "Wait here awhile. Let me go back to the place where God can talk to me, where God will answer me, help me. Deliver me, guide."

As God has blessed others so may we be blessed. Partly, we learn to trust God on the basis of what God has done for others. Do not look over your shoulder to compare yourself with others, but gain strength by knowing that as God has helped others as they passed through the dark, deep, slippery places of life, God was giving us an illustration of God's power to save and bless us.

God means that we should give such strength of knowledge to each other. Therefore, let us face these tests of life with such faith and courage and integrity that some fainting souls will remember our example, go forward knowing they can receive power from God to see it through.

Remember something about God! When we are pressed on every side, swim through the deep waters, and our hearts are heavy and spirits sore, look up, God is there. Never forget that God lives, loves, and leads. God's hand seems strongest when our strength seems weakest. God becomes clearest when troubles press hardest.

On God

God takes no pleasure in our loss and our defeat. This is a new and lofty concept of God. It is a new notion . . . that God is powerful. But does God care? We wonder when we watch a screaming storm come lashing its way through a city, or somewhere when a violent wind is blowing. In our little, dark, muddy corner of the cosmos, where we live out our days and hope and cry and laugh and pray, we wonder if God cares. In our inward parts we know that God does care about our dying and our sorrowing, in our faults and our failures, in our willfulness and our wickedness, in our sickness and our sorrows, God cares.

✧

Let us be reminded that we must view life in all its facets with the eyes of God. Knowing God means, at least in part, seeing things as God sees them. Most people have heard the saying, "looking at the world through rose-colored glasses." But, our task is to look at the world through "God-colored glasses." Both young and seasoned persons will find that life will fall out far more sensibly and far more richly if they read life in every part and time under the light of God.

God wants us to discern the signs of the times. In order to make that possible, our lives must be grounded in an eternal purpose, that even the fitful moods of Earth cannot alter. During these times, even when we are not aware of God's will, some light must break the path. That light comes from God above. God is the master who holds the rudder of our lives, holding us and giving us direction amidst life's raging floods.

☦

God's light is meant for those who have a ford in their minds and a midnight in their hearts. Allow God's light to be a new beginning and break in on your darkened understanding. Life is dark, murky, and foggy until the light of God has been cast over our darkened souls. When that happens we begin to understand the fullness and joy of everything life has to offer.

☦

This is not to say that God does not allow us our hot, fretful moods, when we pound the table before His presence, angry, feeling wronged. . . . It is too much to ask of an everlastingly calm and gentle spirit, even in our dealings with God. . . . God knows our frame and remembers that we are dust. We can bring any mood before God, so long as we cling to our integrity of soul. This God with whom we deal never leaves and never forsakes. . . . Our Calvary may be painful and lonely, our course rough and cruel, but God can and will heal our hurts and soothe our sorrows and turn our grief into glad hosannas.

⁂

Do you not want, long, yearn to move in the God climate? I do yearn to breathe in the God atmosphere, long for that posture of the soul where sin and sense molest no more, heaven comes down our souls to greet, and glory crowns the mercy seat. Do you not long to move in the God way? Let our words and thoughts be God-centered. Let our hopes be God-founded. Let us walk in the God way, talk in the God talk, think in God's thoughts, sing God's songs, and live in God's sight . . . until God is all around us, all over us, all under us, all through us, all behind us, all before us, until God is all in all, and we are caught up to meet God.

⁂

God has focused God's attention on us in such a way that we cannot be forgotten. Our image, our remembrance, is not set up in heaven, as Spurgeon put it, lest we feel, in our poor human way, that God might leave heaven and thus we would be forgotten. God says, "I have graven thee upon the palms of my hands." "I have graven thee"—thy person, thy image, thy case, thy circumstances, thy needs, thy weaknesses, thy wants, and thy works. We are, therefore, wherever God is.

✥

God is our only home. Missing the shelter of God's presence, we are poor wanderers driven hither and yon by changes in circumstances and the relentless onrush of the years. We yearn for some sense of permanence. We want a sense of home that does not change, that stands fast and firm and to which we can go and know that we are midst familiar surroundings and among friendly faces that remain the same.

On God

Our only abiding resting place is God. For God alone remains the same. In God's presence we are fixed for living, prepared for the trials that life most surely brings. Generation after generation has looked to God and found God, and found God a steady rock. It is not just true for any one generation but for all ages. It is true for all times.

I believe we are going to be in the presence of God. Beyond this life, another, far in excess of anything we could describe or perceive. I believe that we can only use these poor earthly examples, like houses, land, automobiles, and churches that are completely inadequate. But these are the best we have, the only things we can use as symbols because we know nothing else. Heaven is close to God Himself, or Herself. That is heaven, existence in the immediate presence of God.

✧ ✧ ✧

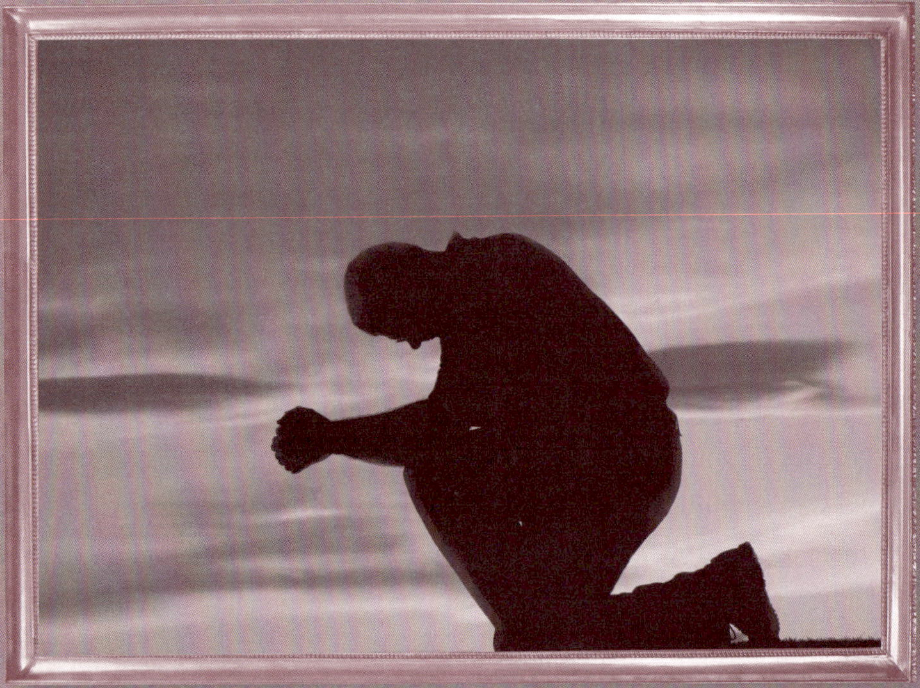

CHAPTER TWO

A GOD WORTH SERVING

"*R*emember the former things of old: for I am God, and there is none else; I am God, and there is none like Me.

"Declaring the end from the beginning, and from ancient times the things that are not yet done, saying, My counsel shall stand, and I will do all My pleasure . . .

"I bring near my righteousness; it shall not be far off, and my salvation shall not tarry: and I will place salvation in Zion for Israel my glory." (Isaiah 46: 9–10, 13)

"Every man has his price" is an ugly and flippant judgment we hear made about men's integrity. In spite of periodic scandals involving people of public trust, something within us makes us believe that every man is not corruptible. "Every man has his price" is open to argument when we see people risking life and facing death in support of their trust and responsibility. I know another sweeping generalization which cannot be successfully contradicted. It is, "Every man has his god." You object as you think of this person or that, whom you have known has never openly confessed Christ as Savior and is not an acknowledged follower of any formal religion, no matter what it may be. Wait a minute! I am not for a moment suggesting that every person has a god which we could call by that name. I am suggesting that every person has an object of worship. Whatever or whoever is my object of final, ultimate, supreme devotion is my god.

Years ago Lewis Mumford said, "Man is incurably religious." I believe this to be true. We are believing, adoring, worshipping creatures. To ascribe final worth to some object is as natural with us as breathing. To pray to, to sing in praise of, to proclaim faith in are instinctive acts with us humans. I believe the anthropologists would say that they have not come across any tribe or race of people anywhere on the face of the earth who could be called a religionless people. I do not know what waits for humans as we open a highway to the planets. Airlines say they are ready to book passengers for flight to the moon. Conceivably, within the lifetime of some of you, this fantastic, incredible idea of commercial flights to the moon will be an everyday occurrence. If there is, as many believe, conscious, rational life on other worlds, I believe travelers to those planets will find humans worshipping. It may be that God as we have known God in Christ has dispatched the Evangel, the Good News, as we know it, to the moon and beyond. I believe that if there is life there, God has put God's mark on it. For I read God has not left Himself without witnesses. On the other hand, if people on the moon have not heard of our God, they will be worshipping something or somebody.

So! The question before us is not whether you will serve a god or not. The question is rather, as a sermon I once tried to preach was titled, is your god worth serving? To serve a god not worth serving is the meaning of idolatry. I thought of people with wooden statues to whom they prayed and who, they believed, could bless or curse them.

This was the earliest form of idolatry. The 46th Chapter of Isaiah pictures God speaking with withering sarcasm of how men make gods. Men lavish gold out of a bag, the Prophet says, and they take their silver and put it on the scales to see if they have enough to finish the god they are making. They go out and hire a goldsmith and ask him to make a god and the goldsmith takes their order and makes them a god. One day those who have contracted for a god call at the goldsmith's shop and ask if their god is ready. The artisan looks on his shelves and sure enough there is an article bearing the name of those making the order. Such a person will pay the goldsmith and take their god and put it on their shoulder and carry the god out into the street on to their houses. Upon arriving home, they take their man-made god and set him up in a prominent place. The god will stay there and cannot move until its worshippers come and move it.

Let us not laugh at this ridiculous characterization I have just made. I knew a man once whose automobile seemed to be his god. This man polished his car daily but did not, as far as I could see, pray daily. He could not stand for a speck of dirt to be on his auto, but there seemed much spotted and unlovely about the owner. In my little town there was a woman whose husband did a type of hard work which made him grimy. This man, out of the fierce labor of his hands, built a lovely home for his wife, at least by the standards of that simple place and far-off day. The woman worshipped the home so much she would not let the man enjoy it who built it for her and forced her husband always to enter through the back door.

Is there anyone here who ever thought clothes were the most important thing in the world? Do you still want to laugh at these simple worshippers? Let me give you some tests of a worthy god before I go on to my main declaration. The gods we make are no good; we need a God who makes us. The gods we carry are no good; we need a God who can carry us. If we must carry our god, it is all so futile since we ought to remember, "We brought nothing into this world and it is certain we can carry nothing out."

The God worth serving is no plaything, but the King of Heaven who sits high and looks low. That note is sounded in my text. The Lord is heard saying, "I am God and there is none other. I declare the end from the beginning. My counsel shall stand." I hear in that the loftiness and majesty of the Eternal God whom we serve. God is High and Holy.

Perhaps we have gone too far with this chumminess with the Almighty. God is the Lord! The King of Heaven and Earth! The King of Glory! I shudder when I hear people talk about "the man upstairs." The true God whom Jesus Christ has shown us is not just some neighbor upstairs. God made the stairs and the house. "The earth is the Lord's and the fullness thereof and they that dwell therein."

There is about the God we serve an awesome majesty. The young Prophet Isaiah said that in the very year King Isaiah died, he saw the Lord sitting upon a throne, high and lifted up, and God's train filled the Temple. Around the throne stood the seraphim, mentioned only once in all Holy Writ. Whether real or symbolic, the literal meaning of "seraph" is "burning," or "fiery."

May I digress long enough to say that the beings, be they real or imaginary, who stand closest to God are glowing and warm and blazing with enthusiasm. There is no ice in God's presence, no chilliness where God reigns, but the closer we get the warmer grow our spirits, the more fervent our devotion. There is about a true Christian a glow and a warmth. I would not give two hoots in hell for a cold, sterile religion. I must return to my thought.

A God Worth Serving

In the Lord's presence, high and lifted up, the Holiest creatures felt humility and reverence and unworthiness and so hid their faces as they shielded their countenances behind the pinions of their mighty wings. We must stop preachers and people, this palsy-walsy sentimentality about the God of Creation's morning. We ought to stop prancing and mincing into God's House at the time of worship with a lot of loud clap-trap and cheap gossip on our lips. "The Lord is in His holy Temple, let all the earth keep silence before Him" . . . God says, "Be still and know that I am God."

The Lord is lofty and above our poor earthly notions and flesh. God is worthy of our service for God is the Creator. I hear God standing, if I may say so, on God's own authority and the Dignity of God's creative glory when people seem to want to turn to lesser deities. Listen to God plead God's own case as the One who hath "measured the waters in the hallow of His hand, and meted out heaven with a span, comprehended the dust of the earth in a measure, and weighed the mountains in scales and the hills in the balances." Let us be done with frivolous and flippant notions of the God we serve. I like old Isaac Watts's words:

"Before Jehovah's awful throne
Ye nations, bow with sacred joy,
Know that the Lord is God alone
He can create, and He destroy."

God is high and holy and yet so close and kind. This is the Paradox of the Godhead. So holy that God cannot abide sin, so loving God cannot see the sinner perish—and so Christ! Consider this other part of the text, "I bring near my righteousness, it shall not be far off, and my salvation shall not tarry: and I will place salvation in Zion for Israel my glory." Someday I am going to preach on God's dilemma between holiness and heartbreak out of which came the Gospel of the seeking, suffering Son of God.

God is near, somebody said, "Nearer than hands and feet." This is the Evangel, the red and silken thread of Good Tidings running through the whole Bible. That's what the Bible is all about: Good News, the best news. Tennyson, so says James Stewart, asked a woman when he arrived from a journey, "What is the News?" "There is only one piece of news. I know Christ died for all." "Well," said Tennyson, "that is old news, and good news, and new news." It is also the best news.

God is near. That is the word of the Bible. Near enough in Eden to be heard by a disobedient Man, "Adam, where art thou?" Near enough as a raging flood swept down on the Creation to warn Noah. Near enough where Enoch walked gently to talk that Patriarch into Eternity. Near enough to signal Abraham until the Father of the Faithful saw the beckoning finger. Near enough to wrestle with Jacob until the morning came. Near enough to blaze before Moses in the plains of Midian and to talk the rebel back to Egypt land and out again. Near enough to be seen as a cloudy pillar before the Pilgrim Host on Israel's march. Near enough to be David's high rock when his heart was overwhelmed. Near enough that we would have to say, "Thou hast been a shelter for me and a strong tower from the enemy."

God is above and yet close. This is the Paradox of the Gospel. At Bethlehem, men saw, as angels gasped, the God of Creation's Morning, the Holy one of Israel, the King of Glory wade into the mud of our common humanity. God is near, I say. At Bethlehem's manger, the Mighty God, Jehovah, the Umpire, the Everlasting Father, the Desire of All Nations, the Original

Cause, The Prime Mover of all that Moves, The Lord God stepped down in this mud and mire. And then on Friday took the foul and ugly load of our sin and shame and put it on His shoulder and climbed a hill and stayed there between a sinning earth and a sorrowing heaven until children gone a long time started looking for Him. God is near. I know God is near. For God walks with me and He talks with me, and He tells me I am His own. God is so near that sometimes reaching out we can almost touch the Lord and so often feel God's power. Yes, God touches me, affects my emotion. Sometimes I can't keep my voice steady and can't keep my eyes dry.

I believe God will always be near. When friends are many, God will be near. When friends are few, God will be near. Near for all tortured souls, near for all lonely hearts, near for all weary Pilgrims. Near for all who sit in the region and shadow of death. Near for all who are wronged and misused. Near for all who mourn and for all who weep in the silent watches of the night. Near when Jordan-flood sounds hoarse in our frightened ears. Near when Death's summons snatches us from our loved ones.

✣ ✣ ✣

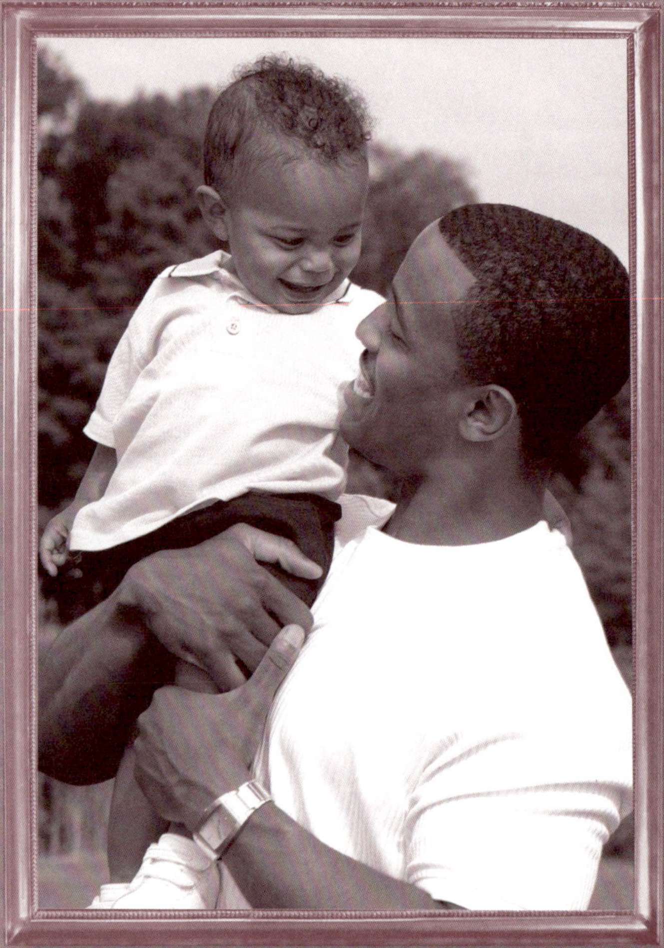

CHAPTER THREE

THE WAY OF LOVE

*B*ut the greatest of these is love. This is a great "Hymn of Love." It tells of the life-bearing message of the permanence of love. Minus love, the insights, which normally reveal the depths of knowledge, are devoid, limpless. All of our philanthropy and all of the works of the sacred martyrs, all of our care for the poor are futile without love. Love is the *summum bonum* of life touched with angelic sweetness, and its strength roars like the mighty thunders of Niagara! Love's figure is firmly fixed and its place securely safe.

✢

Love is beyond any sickly sentimentality but hardheaded, softhearted goodwill. Love is the word of selfless kindliness, God-touched concern. Real love is nobler and higher than other concerns. It goes on, despite barriers, doing its work, bearing its load, climbing its hill, and carrying its cross. It does not look for what it can get but for what it can give. This kind of selfless, seeking goodwill is the essential element of good character. Love is the heartbeat of the Eternal. Love suggests that our hearts have been invaded by a desire to be aggressive, questing and seeking goodwill. We can trust this kind of love because it is lasting, rugged, and endures the test.

✢

Love is our central power. Love becomes our motivation and the center of emotion. We are directed by love not because of praise or blame, credits or cures, promotion or punishment.

✢

Love is tough, determined, discerning, and undiscourageable. Love causes us to love anyhow! It can suffer a long time. Love is not competitive. It does not envy another. Love has no illusions and lives in no fool's paradise. Love does not care about our past, but embraces us as we are. The love of which I speak is humble; it is not puffed up. This kind of love is not ugly and aggressive; it does not behave itself unseemly. You cannot upset it; it is not easily provoked. In sickness and sorrow, in pain and privations, love never fails.

Love defines the basic structure of the universe.
Doubtless, various levels of reality exist but at the bedrock
of reality is this goodness; there is a mercy that is all based on love.
Love is the essence of what holds creation together. Cast away
the wonders, energies, and powers of this world at the bottom of things.
At the heart of it all exists the great secret: Love.

This kind of love must find expression in the world. As Michelangelo offered the genius of his sculpture to express his love; as Handel offered his Messiah to show forth his love and adoration; as the great cathedrals of Notre Dame, Cologne, and Westminster all attest to a moving, adoring love, so must we express our love.

Love stays on when everything else has left. Love abides! It keeps its vigil around sickbeds and slips through the bars of prison cells. Love stays on! It defies shame and disdains disgrace and believes in us anyhow. It bears pain and endures sorrow, and climbs dark hills. Love lasts when death is passed and the night is come. Love abides, when life has fled and the pulse is stilled, and our homes are empty. This love is hard to march up to, but it demands that we come up to the hard, crippling facts of life, with deep confidence that this love will never let us go. Even beyond all other considerations we dare to believe that this kind of love is the test of life.

✢

Love: Our new-world optimism and Hollywood preoccupation with romantic feelings has taken from this old word its affirmative toughness. It means an enlightened, aggressive, relentless will for the good of all people. Love is not the sugary, sentimental, soft thing of which we think when the word " love" is uttered. Even when we accept the meaning of the word, we are likely to believe that our commitment to love one another is private and individual: a cup of cold water to those who thirst, and a piece of bread to those who hunger, one by one as we have opportunity. To love one another does involve our personal relations vitally and inescapably, for gift without the giver is bare.

☦

We have not yet been willing to throw into our great, massive, structural arrangements of society the commandment to love one another. To be aggressively committed to the good of all people in our businesses and in our industries seems to most of us a little too large an order. To be stubbornly determined that our arrangements of government shall be marshaled to the true benefit of all people seems to so many of us a little too grandiose for us to conceive. To be led of love is to have an audacious optimism, realistic and clear-eyed, in those who surrender to love, to love one another.

FAITH IN THE FIRE

―――――

Love outlasts the acids of change and the corrosion of time.
Love stands straight and secure midst the storms and floods in
which other virtues have shaken and stopped and succumbed.
Love is a great quality; it gives purpose to the lives of people and
declares to them that there is a land where their worthiest beliefs are
brought to pass. Love gives luster to tomorrow and fills the future with
promise. Love will keep a person marching when strength is gone.

―――――

Love is a stubborn thing. Love is perhaps the most persistent thing on Earth. Love shoulders up its load and keeps on climbing, though the ascent is steep and dizzying. I say this with an admiration for the believing stubborn quality of love. This love is a mother's love that will put tears of great sorrow in her eyes and immeasurable joy in her heart.

We must be able to see love on a human level. Love will make parents hold on to their children through all kinds of shame and rebuffs. Love will propel busy and modern people out of graves where even the lettering on tombstones have been almost erased by the ravages of the passing years of storms and sun. Love gives in memory and abides in the hearts of those who are touched.

※

We are creatures made to love, to give our hearts in trust and surrender one to the other. Withholding love and trust are unnatural impulses. This capacity for love opens us to so many hurts and to so many struggles; bitter, anguished, raw, bleeding suffering. The moment you give your trust in friendship or love, you open yourself, expose yourself to betrayal and humiliation. Have you not seen such love and trust rejected and trampled upon? I will not peer down the street where some lament the indifference of others and whose wail is fashioned out of their love.

Love of the Eternal is no dead-end street. Love leads us out into the workaday world. It is not cloistered or quarantined. We love the Eternal first with all our hearts and our neighbors as ourselves. Love takes an interest in those around us. Every person becomes the focus of our love. We must love people—young people and senior saints, creatures, the Earth, wish them well, seek to do them good, even at great cost and pain.

God could have found so many ways to spread the Gospel of God's love. God might have written God's love on the leaves of the trees, and blowing winds would have sent news of deliverance, and redemption far and wide. God might have written God's love in the skies and in the rising sun so that humanity, looking upward, could have read the message. God might have made the ocean sing God's love and nightingales to chant it. Yet, God's love is known in us.

God's love has been operating far back in the misty, nebulous, indescribable non-regions of eternity. Even then God's love was at work. When God loved us there was nothing to love except His own intention. This is our ground for believing that this universe is keyed to love. First of all things was God's love, at the beginning of all things is God's love. Out of the farthest precincts and outposts of God's creation, love is central. I do not know how far ten billion light-years are located in distance, but God's love touches that part of God's creation, for God first loved us.

✜

Dr. George Buttrick, erstwhile pastor of the famed Madison Avenue Presbyterian Church of New York City, once told the story of a nun, in all likelihood a nurse, who was seen by a man working on a repulsive sore on the leg of a man. As the pus oozed from the sore and the nun patiently and expertly treated the rotting flesh, an onlooker said to her, "I would not do that for a million dollars." She looked up quietly, smiled a little, and said as she continued working on the sore, "I would not either!" All that we do, we do for love!

William J. Clinton Presidential Library

CHAPTER FOUR

CULTURE AND POLITICS

The word "Thanksgiving" appears in both the first and second testaments of the Bible, but is not one of the canonical or "appointed" feasts in the first testament, nor does it rise to what may be called a canonical observance in the second. Nevertheless, Thanksgiving Day in America rises to an American religious "holyday," sanctified by the American experience from the founding of the nation through our Civil War when President Lincoln associated the day with the nation's baptism in blood and its "new birth of freedom," as he put it. It is interesting that his declaration of a day of Thanksgiving came almost within a month of the date when his historic address at Gettysburg Cemetery was delivered. Thankfulness belongs to our human emotional equipment. Both the theistic believer and non-believer must look beyond oneself for the satisfaction of that instinct. The theistic adherent is spared a daunting incertitude in this regard. Almost all others are thankful—but to what? Or whom?

I believe that anyone has a right to express his or her personal religious views at any time, most appropriately when the expression is not obviously aimed at garnering votes. In addition, I believe that "personal religious views" are infinitely more appropriate if they result from personal religious practice, which is not merely of the moment.

During my years in the Democratic Party in New York, it was said during election time of one politician that he was not what he looked like and he looked like what he was not. And neither one made very little difference.

My closest living friend is Vernon Jordan, who is managing director of Lazard Brothers international investment firm. As a boy, Mr. Jordan was working as a houseboy, so to speak, for a wealthy member of the Atlanta meritocracy—the people of wealth and influence. Vernon was caught reading in the library of this gentleman. The owner came in and found him reading and was astonished, dumbfounded. He said to his family at dinner that evening, and Vernon overheard it, "Vernon can read," which was a disappointment to the family, which this gentleman represented. The family was aghast at the idea that this little black youngster could actually read.

✧

The American mass communications networks honor religion in the same manner which prompted Jesus to say " . . . this people honoreth me with their lips, but their heart is far from me" (Mark 7:6). The prophet Isaiah much earlier reported that this same word was the indictment made by God (Isaiah 29:13). The media reminds one of an incident in which, it was said, a religious procession led with the Crucifix passed along the streets of Paris. Voltaire, the philosopher and Deist, who was not noted for religious practice, stood watching. As the Crucifix passed, Voltaire removed his hat. "I did not know you to be religious," said a friend. Replied the skeptic Voltaire: "I am not. We salute but we do not speak."

✛

People in media shy away from any reference to religion; there is a general embarrassment in America about admitting publicly any relationship to God. For instance, if an athlete being interviewed mentions his or her relation to God, there is a nonplussed expression on the face of the media interviewer and then the subject is quickly changed.

It may be—though one hesitates to say it—that public figures, preachers and politicians in particular, have so wantonly exploited religion for personal gain and to cloak the most ungodly purposes that what ought to be the most precious aspect of life, proudly held, becomes a shame and a stench in society.

✛

Culture and Politics

The price we pay for God's love and respect for us in making us free is the kind of senseless tragedy, which happened at Virginia Tech. If we had been created with no choice as to our actions, then the shooting could not have occurred, but then neither could the wonderful achievements of the human spirit. We will hear again the tired old refrain, "Guns do not shoot and kill people, people shoot and kill people." To that must be added, "People without guns do not shoot and kill people." The external reason—guns—for this horror can be removed by legislation. The internal reason for this tragedy, admittedly more important, can be removed by training almost from the cradle, which says that only God gives life and it is infinitely precious; too precious to be assaulted by mean public and private discourse and by a culture which sneers at our spiritual roots and which welcomes dehumanizing language as normal, be it in private conversation or over the national airwaves. The latter is more lethal since it can claim an infinitely larger hearing. Finally, our society is doomed unless religious pulpits, public platforms, college lecterns, communications media, and, indeed, all of us decide that we will leave the sewer in our thoughts and conversation and turn upward toward the stars. That will fit us better, since God has made us "a little lower than the angels" (Psalm 8:5; Hebrews 2:7).

☩

Yes, Satan exists. That ominous figure can be seen on Wall Street, operating where greed threatens the nation. That ugly figure exists on Main Street where we buy the lie that our whole economy can and will correct itself. Satan exists on your street and mine, tempting us, more times than not successfully, with the sugar-coated fatal poison that we are well able to handle our affairs without God directing and determining the course we take. Our old enemy, dressed in dinner jacket, evening gown, sports attire, or without garment, is ever present.

☩

The issue of disarmament (a nuclear-free world) is first and foremost a religious issue. One has only to read Matthew 5:9, "Blessed are the peacemakers: for they shall be called the children of God." One fully expects the usual anti-Obama cabal inevitably to be critical of his efforts for a nuclear-free world, partly, if not wholly, for other reasons. These gloomy naysayers need some advice. Those who cannot support President Obama because he inherited his blackness from his father surely ought to support him because he inherited his whiteness from his mother. Then, Hail to the Chief, our first completely American president. What America has carried on its coinage is coming true—*E Pluribus Unum.* God be praised!

☩

The nation was consumed with the argument as to whether everyone should have the benefit of health insurance even if the federal government had to pay for it. A great Christian denomination met for four or five days and did not ever mention the need of health. Is that "good religion," as our forefathers sang?

☩

How could the nation be consumed with discussion, fevered sometimes, as to whether there should be health insurance for everybody? How could it be that none of our civic organizations was recorded as being on record for or against?

※

In the second Genesis account of creation (Genesis 2), the Creator settled His creatures in a setting, which the Creator called "good" and "very good." In that setting, represented as a "garden," the tenants were to "dress it and keep it." It is an interesting aside, as Alexander Maclaren pointed out, that the woman formed was not created out of the man's feet, thus to be trampled upon, nor from his head, thus to be his superior, but from his side that they might walk, hand in hand, together. People of faith are under covenant, or contract, to "dress" the earth and to "keep" it, not by greed or stupidity to darken its skies and to pollute its waterways. Failure to keep the terms of our creation means that the covenant-breakers forfeit the right to occupy what their blundering selfishness has fouled and corrupted. Is this to be our human fate, now being adumbrated by scientific findings?

※

The wide attention given to Mother Teresa's doubt about God and Christ represents an almost universal struggle, which goes on in most of us who are believers. Faith and doubt are the two sides of the same religious experience. Even Jesus felt that abandonment on Calvary about the presence of God, though at the last He said that He was able to give Himself into the hands of God with a blessed finality. An example might be a silver dollar held up to the light. Viewing the coin from its top, one sees brightness and clarity. The bottom side of the coin is in shadows, away from the light. But it is the same coin. There would be no doubt if doubt did not have something, which makes doubt possible. What makes doubt real is faith—the ultimate capacity of the human spirit.

⁜

The seven deadly sins are almost all related to one another. For instance, one lusts because one has gluttony, which is another form of greed. In our current society, greed is the chief sin, but it is a child of lust for authority and supremacy. The nation's future rests on whether we can free ourselves of inordinate greed, which is twin, if not parent, to lust, anger, and gluttony. Greed has corrupted our practice of Christian faith with the heresy that God exists to satisfy our lusts and gluttony.

FAITH IN THE FIRE

✦

Government has a right to attack *Roe v. Wade* only when it guarantees that the fetus will have a quality education, adequate food and housing, quality health care, and a favorable community in which to advance. Anything short of this is infanticide in stages and wanton hypocrisy.

If association with someone establishes guilt or a similar condition, doctors who associate with sick people must be sick. Lawyers spending time with suspected criminals must be suspected of crime. Jesus was said to be a friend of sinners (Matthew 11:19, Luke 7:34), then he must be suspected of being a sinner. People with ugly purposes need to beware of conclusions.

It may be said that these "Representatives of the United States of America," as they are referred to in the Declaration of Independence, came closest to the spirit of Jesus Christ by not being dogmatic and intolerant in their writings. Some latter-day bigots, masquerading as Christians, might well take lessons from them in this regard.

Perhaps all of us should remember a word, which first appeared in another generation in a midwestern newspaper, which said, "There is so much bad in the best of us and so much good in the worst of us that it hardly behooves any of us to talk about the rest of us."

Cancer needs more severe and radical treatment than does a simple pimple. The question of race is not a marginal, minor feature of our history. One of the participants in the Constitutional Convention observed that there was a sleeping serpent under the table where the founders met. He meant "Race."

If the historical Jesus were running for our United States presidency, He would be a "Demopublican," combining what is affirmative in both parties, rejecting shrillness, anger, posturing, and denouncing the corruption made inevitable by the necessary scrounging for money, much to the anger, I am sure, of television and newspaper profit-makers, to say nothing of political hangers-on, and talking heads prostituting their voices for profit. In the case of abortion or the death penalty or war, He would place the work of every individual soul before God above all considerations. I think He would also be assassinated, lynched, or, if you prefer, crucified as before.

✣

Rev. Jeremiah Wright's preaching, and what should be Senator Obama's response as a parishioner, engages our American media understandably. The matter really comes down to several considerations. A pastor preaching and pastoring is not called on to be a mirror in which the congregation can identify themselves. He or she is called on to be a kind of clear window through which congregants are called to see the vision of what they ought to be and do individually and collectively.

Culture and Politics

Is everyone entitled to freedom of worship? Is there a religious test by which one is deemed suitable for public office? This was the question faced by John Kennedy as he sought the presidency. I am a Baptist. Every Baptist, at least those who would be true to their core Baptist beliefs, would insist on freedom to worship or not to worship according to conscience. A corollary of that position would be no religious test for public office. Opposition for these principles is to commit treason against the idea of America and its political creed.

⁂

A cardinal constitutional principle has to do with freedom of worship, as that precious provision is stated in Amendment 1 of our Constitution. In addition, a basic American right is to be free from religious tests in order to hold public office. That goes back before the Constitution to a basic Virginia statute. Those who attack any American citizen about this pivotal American privilege of freedom of worship commits treason against the American idea in history. Do such hired voices really care about religious or patriotic concerns? If they do not, then they are political and vocal prostitutes.

Dr. Peter Holmes is a Canadian pastor of the Yorkminster Baptist Church in Toronto. My friend Jerome Washington was there, and Dr. Holmes, who had also pastored in Montreal, told of how he and his wife vacationed in Florida where a man asked him about the health plan in Canada. Dr. Holmes said, "It is wonderful. We are having a wonderful experience with it." The man said, "Oh, no. It couldn't be. It's socialism." The more Holmes tried to explain how fine it was, and the more determined the man became that it is a failure, the clearer it was that he was talking to a dummy.

I was born in 1918, not far removed from the occasion when President Theodore Roosevelt entertained Booker T. Washington at lunch in the White House. My elders talked with great feeling about that honor. Now a person of their color is scheduled to eat, sleep, and live in that same White House.

What an apparently providential confluence of circumstances brought this to pass: the long, often violent night of a people's sojourn in this land and their refusal to let hope die; a political disaster of eight years standing; an apparently endless war in a strange, distant land; the near collapse of a great nation's economy; the candidacy of one whose years emphasize his mortality joined to a running mate of dubious credentials; the dim awareness of American people that the idea of this nation is not yet fleshed out; the collapse of a wealthy, well-trained opponent due to marital indiscretion; and the appearance on the public scene of a figure of becomingly mixed parentage with impeccable academic credentials joined to a mystically compelling personality and with a mate of charm and culture. Therefore, God be praised, Barack Obama! Let all see the hand of the God of History at His work in this matter.

✣

Presidents, too, can go to hell here and hereafter if they allow their souls to shrivel and decay with hubris and starvation of the spirit. Secular office, no matter its height or esteem, is no substitute for worship in a community of faith. Our president, faced with incredibly complex issues presented to him by the past, needs to find a church where he can be accepted as a soul in need of spiritual encouragement. Also, all of us, president and citizens, will profit from reading the Reverend John Winthrop's sermon delivered to Puritans aboard the *Arbella* in 1630 nearing these shores to establish the American nation. Winthrop said, "If we shall deal falsely with our God and shame many of God's Worth servants [we shall] cause their prayers to be turned into curses upon us. . . . We shall surely perish out of this good land whither we pass over this vast sea to possess it."

✢

One does not want to think that the complexion of our present President of the United States has anything to do with the opposition to the proposed changes in our health care legislation. Or is this a revival of the discounted, disgraced McCarthy era? Some of the anger is fueled by the

Culture and Politics

kind of misanthropes on television and elsewhere who express themselves by such statements as "Give me back my country." "What un-American adventurer has taken the country?"

*President Barack Obama receives
approximately 38 threats on his life each day,
1¼ threats per hour. At this rate, the man says he will receive
210 threats a week, 840 threats a month,
10,080 threats a year, and 40,320 threats in his first term.*

I think many Americans do not realize the implications of a representative from South Carolina, named Joe Wilson, calling out in the joint meeting of Congress on the evening of 09/09/09, I guess. As the President spoke, a voice rang out, "You lie," which was never heard before in the history of Congress in a joint session. But people do not realize that there was a time when a black man could be called a liar or could be seen as a liar, and black people would laugh. But now, when you call the President of the United States, who happens to be black, a liar, you are insulting the United States in the halls of Congress. What does that mean for the future of the country, for the confidence in the nation's elected offices?

✣

In the morning fresh of September 16, the congressional hearing of the Republican Party came about from the outcry about Representative Joe Wilson's epithet hurled at President Obama as being "a liar," and said that it is "a witch hunt." He did not say that the witch has been found and now reprimanded by Congress.

✣

It is reported that a man who purports to be a minister and pastor named Stephen Anderson, who pastors what is called The Faithful Word of God Church, has said in a prayer about President Obama, "Break his teeth, O God, and his mouth, and I am going to pray for him and pray for his wife, Michelle, and pray for his children, (and maybe more urgently) I am going to pray for our nation." This is a nation which calls itself Christian.

FAITH IN THE FIRE

---

*If President Obama is looked upon
as a divine creature then he is in direct succession
to another divine creature, as many people thought, George W. Bush.
The truth is we all are children of God and therefore,
members of a divine family. Presidents are expected to be
spiritual leaders as we all are expected to be, being Children of God.*

There are those who dislike, who hate President Obama because his father was African and black or who love President Obama because his mother was Anglo-Saxon and white. Presto, we all have something to love and something to hate in our President. All hail to President Obama, a true American, or halfway, either way at least. We all have something to hate and something to love. Hail to our President, a true African, and a true American.

✣

Some of the anger expressed on the floor of the joint session of the United States Congress indicates an unwillingness to accept the verdict at Appomattox Court House that ended the Confederacy. Some of this opposition, of course, is due to a normal fear of change, and therefore understandable.

✣

There was a pastor in New Orleans named John Mark who was at that time, not too long after slavery, the only person who could write. He was Secretary of the First District Baptist Association, and whenever something went contrary to John Mark's idea, he would walk out of the association and that would force it to close because nobody else could read or write.

✣

Remember the quotation by Tom Oliphant who covered Senator Ted Kennedy's career for four decades at *The Boston Globe?* Oliphant asked the late Senator, "Where does this rabid concern about poverty come from?" Senator Kennedy's reply was, "Have you never read the New Testament?" The final judgment upon such people is that they are like wolves in sheep's clothing, posing as true Americans. Such people are traitors to the American creed, as are those who reject the findings of the New Testament, even though they call themselves Christians.

⸸

We broke it, so we have a moral obligation to help put Iraq together again. In the rebuilding of Iraq we need to take the role of partners rather than masters.

⸸ ⸸ ⸸

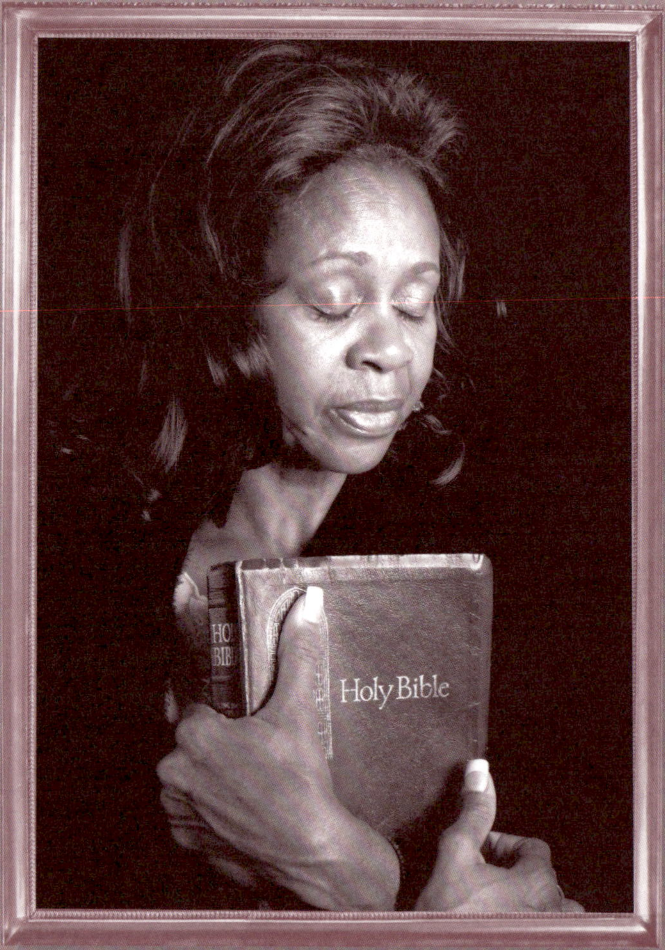
Holy Bible

CHAPTER FIVE

EMBRACING HOPE

*H*ope is joyful and conquers the wistful spirit. It faces our trying days of unbelief and cold practicality with a magnificent If, the mightiest Maybe, and a grand Perhaps. This is hope and it exists outside us and beyond this life. This is the incurable optimism that flows like a spring from the human heart.

✣

What keeps us united as a people? Hope. Hope gives strength to justice and human dignity. For those who have faced indignity and discrimination, hope encourages us to give ourselves to waiting for the ever clearer and coming day where human brotherhood will not die, and color and creed will no longer matter. This is the hope, which binds our nation together.

Hope gives purpose to human life and declares to them that there is a place where their worthiest beliefs are brought to pass. Hope gives luster to tomorrow and fills the future with promise. Hope will keep us marching when strength is gone. Hope speaks to souls when we are at a loss. Hope declares that a person who has taken blow after blow is still solvent and in business.

Hope looks at gloom and misery and lifts the weary heart to the mountain peak of living. Hope keeps whispering midst the waste-howling wilderness that there is a better country on ahead. Hope keeps saying when we are climbing high mountains that the road levels off ahead. Hope can make hospital beds bearable and prison bars endurable. In the darkest valleys and along the bitterest journeys, hope keeps saying press on. Hope survives the wrecks and ruins of time. Hope always tells us there is something better.

"Hope deferred maketh the heart sick," wrote a wise man. When we are ready to conclude that there is no God anywhere and hope is dead, we ought to consider how it has been with us in the past, through whatever difficulties we have somehow been led. God's voice rises like a trumpet of doom and hope midst the scattered dreams and sagging morale of God's own people. This is the blessed hope of people of faith. Among the din and strife of our time, nothing is clearer than the truth that God is our hope.

☩

Life without hope is despair. Too many of us come to that valley of hopelessness too quickly and too easily. It is easy to throw up the hands and to issue a bullet in defeat. It does not take any great patience or any remarkable courage to decide that all is lost, and neither toil nor praying will save the day. There is a virtue in holding on. Hope says we should hold on just a little while longer. What fame or fortune could many have attained if they had stayed on and held on a little while longer. We often give up too easily and it is a temptation that all of us have to face.

At the same time, there is such a thing as real honest-to-goodness hopelessness. There are some ugly facts we have to face in the living of our days. There are some disappointments that cut us deep and sore. There is no use making believe that nothing is really bad, that it is all in our minds. There are some terrible experiences, tear-forcing reversals, heartbreaking events, hurting betrayals that are real. People do say some cutting, unkind things. We are all tempted to despair and with good reason. It is the message of real hope that a heart can hold on, and a spirit can smile in the darkest hours if the soul has hope.

The star of hope shines clearly only in the nighttime; the glowworm glows only in darkness; the jeweler puts its finest stones on black velvet backgrounds. Though we are in one place in life hitherto is what we should hitch on to, out of the past to give hope in the future. With all our strength, all our light, all our help, let us hope. We have one more faith, more prayer, more love, more hope.

Hope does not wear out and exhaust. Hope imagines a new day. It has an "about to be" quality; a new thing, a new notion can happen at any moment. Hope carries a sense of excitement. A kind of suppressed trembling exists, knowing that something spectacular can occur in an instant. This is the quality of freshness that makes life so exciting. Every day there is a chance to walk anew, to hear another word, to pit our might against the strength of this world, to run and not be weary, to walk and not faint. Hope does not get tired. Hope continues beyond our capacity to endure and beyond our ability to understand. Hope waits so we wait until hope turns into action. That belief in the "Until" is our hope.

⁜

A hope in us, which is almost always so fragile that it seems about to flicker out, flames up with warmth and brightness. We know some of the wistful hope in Robert Ingersoll when, standing at the grave of his brother, he said, "Life is a narrow vale between the cold and barren peaks of two eternities. . . . From the voiceless lips of the unreplying dead comes no word; but in the night of death, hope sees a star, and listening love can hear the rustling of a wing."

Hope calls us to live in the world where we must find some satisfaction and sustaining meaning as to why we are here. What is our purpose? Hope says that truth can be known, honesty may be found! Hope says goodness and kindness will prevail! Thou despair can be our lot; hope springs eternal in the human heart. The spiritless and pessimists must know that with hope tomorrow can be a better and brighter day. The purpose of which we are will be made plain if we hope until our purpose is known.

⁂

Hope gives us the promise of peace, the vision of a better land. The limitations of sight will not dull the vision of hope and the acids of modernity will not corrode it. Their vision may dim but will not die. Hope and the goals and gift of hope are our universal desire.

⁂

Embracing Hope

Belief beyond despair is hope. In the midst of wickedness and weakness, we must hope. Hope in the midst of faults and failures, hope in the midst of disaster. When facing death with its foul despair, hope. Not allowing this mean world to have the last word, hope. If you are facing illness and need healing, hope! When all the world's dark disasters come, every enemy stands against us, every stormy wind blows, and every troubled time seems near, hope! Youth and energy may pass, friends fail, troubles rise, scenes fail, comrades die, health may fail, but hope!

One may ask, "What hope do we have when all seems lost? When evil seems to win?" What hope do we have, when truth is slain, death seems to reign, faith appears dead, mercy is a prisoner, grace a captive, and terror abides? How does hope live in these circumstances? Hope encourages our faith and fight in these situations. When all seems lost, hope inspires us to continue. Hope calls upon a higher and greater power that sustains us into the storm and through the storm.

☦

We must see ourselves as seers of hope. Looking at our circumstance and that of others, we can envision a mature hope. In this, we can be an encouragement to those we know. We can lift their spirits beyond the days of discouragement and uncertainty. A hope that can imagine the far side of tragedy, terror, trouble, and tribulation, this hope does not create a Pollyanna or Hollywood fairy tale. Yet, it would have us believe that after hurting comes healing. Those things, which are ugly and intolerable, will have something wonderful built atop them. Beyond our dark valleys we shall enter into sunshine, beautiful garments will replace tattered clothes, the hurts of our lives are healed, and wounds are bound to make us whole. The very desires of our hearts are rewarded beyond our capacity to ask or think. We see what is before us knowing something better exists. This is hope.

☦ ☦ ☦

Time & Life Pictures/Getty Images. Photographer Ted Thai

CHAPTER SIX

THE BASIS OF A CHRISTIAN'S COURAGE

"Being entrusted, then, by God's mercy with this ministry, we do not play the coward." (II Corinthians 4:1, Knox translation)

"Therefore, being enjoyed in this service and being mindful of the mercy which has been shown us, we are not cowards." (II Corinthians 4:1, Weymouth translation)

✧

It is my conclusion, based on all these years' experience, that the Christian has the wording best a dozen times when it comes to courage. This is not to say that godless people are cowards. It is to say that their brand of courage is wintry and cold, while the Christian's brand of courage is warm and sunlit. The unbelieving person's bravery is likely to be either a reckless, devil-may-care kind of daring or a grim, tight-lipped, frowning fatalism, a kind of "whatever will be will be." On the other hand, the Christian is likely to be the kind of person who looks reality in the face and knows that severe reverses can occur and terrible things can leap suddenly out of the darkness to almost tear the soul to pieces. In the Christian Fellowship, a believer has seen just this happen to his brothers and sisters. The Christian knows that there are awful temptations, awful snares, pitfalls, and an enemy is trying to pull us under. He sings, "Sure, I must fight if I would reign." He or she knows life is hard, but if in all these years I have not misread the evidence, Christian people do have a great, sunlit bravery in the face of trials and disappointments, discouragements and slander.

Paul says it clearly to the Corinthians. And you had better not question this man's courage. He campaigned in enemy territory for twenty and more years in the name of Jesus Christ. I do not want to have to submit his credentials of courage. They are spread on the pages of the New Testament. In Acts 9, there is the record of this man's courage. In Damascus Paul's enemies set up a watch at the gates of the city to prevent his escape. In order to move out on the mission of Christ, the trapped Apostle got in a basket and by night his friends let him down by the wall. Frightened? He turns up a few days later in Jerusalem looking for a chance to tell men about His Lord and Savior, Jesus Christ. That same chapter said that at Jerusalem, Paul "spoke boldly in the name of the Lord Jesus." Once, he was stoned in Lystra for upholding the Gospel, dragged out of the city and left for dead. The next day Paul turned up in Derbe, some twenty or thirty miles away, preaching Jesus Christ. Look at him again far on toward the end. He is a prisoner in Rome awaiting execution. He is not whining or crying, but says, "The time of my departure is at hand. I am now ready to be offered up." This man says that our Christian courage, rooted in what we are doing and in the mercy of God who has called us, shows forever. As Monsignor Ronald Knox translates this passage, "Being entrusted, then, by God's mercy with this ministry, we do not play the coward," or as Dr. Weymouth translates it, "Therefore, being engaged in this service and being mindful of the mercy which has been shown us, we are not cowards."

It is my testimony based upon thirty years of close observation and ministry in all kinds of terrible circumstances that Christian people, by and large, show a rare, sunny, bright, hopeful, unbuttered courage in all sorts of circumstances. Now, I know that many people believe and a lot of so-called militants loudly announce any and every where they can get a hearing that Christianity is too soft for our time. It is weak and effeminate, what with its constant prattle about love and pity and forgiveness and good will. They tell us that what we need is grit in the craw, to roll the eyes, frown the face, look mean, talk tough, get out and fight, and by force of arms bring down all that is wrong. Yet, in the testing, in the heat and fire of life's bitter struggle, I have not seen weakness in Christians, but a great courage, a firmness to face what must be faced and in the name of God to carry on with hope and faith.

Paul says that the Christian has courage because he is in Service in the Lord's Cause, "Entrusted with this ministry . . . being engaged in this service." We may well take courage for this cause of Jesus Christ as right. A lot of the ugly changes hurled at the church are hurled by people who want the people of God to be doing what the critic wants them to do. Why can't all of those outside the church, or inside it who believe that the church is all wrong, get out and go on and start their organization to do what they think ought to be done?

It is an old charge which goes back to Jesus. Believer, the criticism of Jesus was that he did not do the big, bold things which the times demanded. As Dr. Gossip puts it, "Indignantly, they who had, at first, been much attracted to Him came to the conclusion that there was nothing in Him. Look at the state of affairs round us, they cried angrily—how Rome grinds us down, how these publications fatten on our misery, how poor and desperate we are. And He has hardly a word to say about all that, but keeps talking, talking, talking about our hearts and sins. Our hearts are all right; there is nothing wrong with us; but we have never had a chance and can't have until this whole system of things that is choking us is shattered. And they turned away."

But Christ kept on His own course. Now let us look at the record. There were armed rebellions against Rome by weak and divided nations. These adventures usually ended in abject humiliation and defeat. Christ followed His own way and refused to be cajoled aside to win anybody's favor or applause. And what happened? Old Rome with all of its armies and mighty power bowed down at last at the foot of the Cross. The Galilean had won.

And we are on the right track. What we need to be doing is more of what the Lord of the Church told us to do. We are told to remind men that righteousness exalteth a nation, but sin, all kinds of sin—racism, war, economic exploitation, job discrimination—are all a reproach to any people. The Church cannot prescribe what must be done in exact formula—but we can make people see and feel that these evils are here and will destroy us. We are here to remind the world that men, truly changed, will change conditions which stifle the human dream.

We are on the right course. Jesus Christ is right. No other way is ever going to win.

We can have courage for we are on the winning side. Far from giving up, we are to respond to trouble and trials as the young Hebrew lad, Daniel, did when the storms of criticism, slander, and conspiracy broke around his head. Darius of Babylon made Daniel, the Hebrew exile, one of his own representatives to whom the princes of Babylon were to report. The princes grew jealous, for there are always those who do not like to see another rise to success. They plotted on Daniel and decided they would use his religious faith against him. They got the King to make a decree that no man in the Kingdom should call on any god, only on the King for thirty days. A kind of suspension of religious devotion. The King signed the decree.

What would Daniel do when he heard of the decree? The Scripture says that when Daniel knew that the writing was signed, he did not close his prayer shop; he went into his house, opened his windows toward Jerusalem, kneeled down on his knees, and prayed and gave thanks to God, as he did, get this, aforetimes. The Christian does not have to worry. We are on the right side. We have to keep on with this ministry, serving our God, praying, singing, preaching, going forth to try to make the world a little better, voting in conscience and prayer, trying to strengthen our families. Soon this storm will be passing over. Soon this moment of terror will flee away like the dew before the summer's sun. Soon the madness of this period will slip away.

Not only are we in the right service and on the right track, but, as Paul said why he never became a coward, God's mercy has been to see us and will make everything all right. Mercy, God's way of dealing with us according to God's goodness; mercy, that old word of the Bible, which means those outward acts of deliverance and keeping by God in which God expresses His love for us. Mercy is love coming to our rescue. Mercy is God's compassion with overalls on. Mercy is God's care with its traveling shoes coming to help us. Mercy is God's pure love stepping down into the mud to pluck us clear of the miry clay.

We don't have to be afraid and I am not afraid. I'm not saying that this is not a hard fight. It is. There are things in this life that will make your heart bleed and your eyes water with tears and your spirit feel so sore inside of you. We can't protect ourselves against everything, but God's mercy can help us. Sometimes something strikes at us when we are not aware that any blow is being aimed at us. We are slandered and lied on and it hurts and we can't protect ourselves. But God's mercy comes around and warns us when we are unaware. Sometimes we can't defend ourselves, but God's mercy knocks on our door and tell us, "Be still! I'll fight your battle. Be still my soul, the Lord is on thy side." Leave to thy God to honor and provide. In every changing, the faithful will remain. Thy God doth understand. Be still, my soul. And He will warn when unseen danger comes, protecting us from those who would do us ill.

Oh, yes, the contrary winds do blow and sometimes our feet seem to be snatched from beneath us by the swift currents and whirling eddies, but we

The Basis of a Christian's Courage

may have courage; for God's mercy still stands. It will be hard, but not too hard. We will get hurt, but not mortally wounded. Paul said, "We are troubled on every side, yet not distressed; we are perplexed, but not in despair; persecuted, but not forsaken; cast down, but not destroyed; weeping, but not as those without hope." Be of good courage, Believer, the Lord is on your side. When deceitful men and tempting devils have done all they can do, God will be a wall round about you.

✣ ✣ ✣

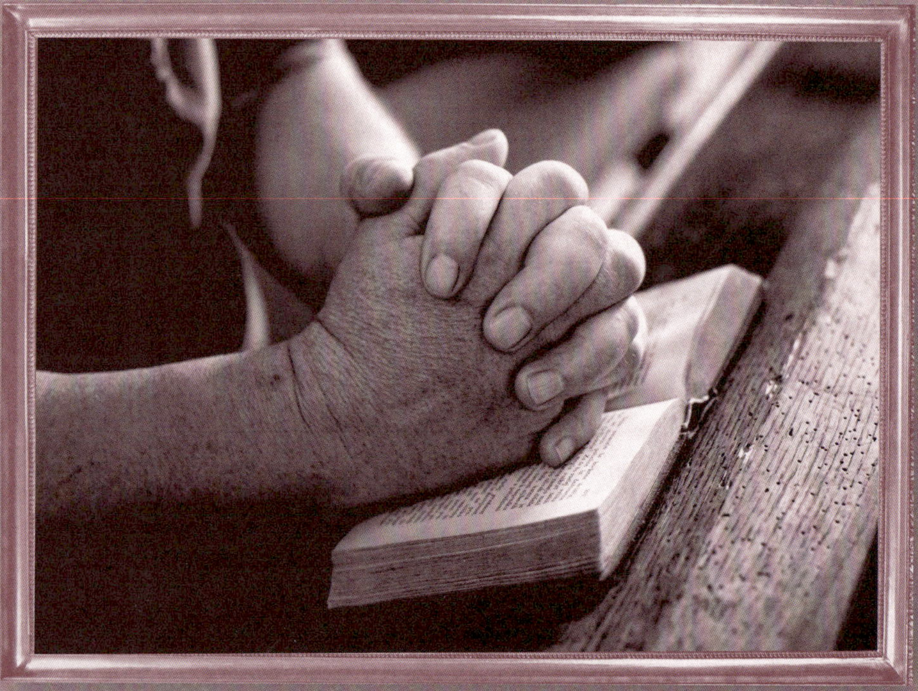

CHAPTER SEVEN

HAVE PATIENCE

Patience belongs to the language of faith. Patience is God's nature. A psalmist saw it uniquely when he penned these words: "A thousand years in thy sight are but as yesterday when it is past, and as a watch in the night." That is God's way. A faithless patience is foolishness and an assault on human wisdom. A person cannot wait in quiet confidence unless that person has something to wait with. The writer pictures himself holding on through the long night, while others are asleep and the night moves on leaden wings. Waiting on God is difficult. We have not been promised a smooth voyage, but God does promise us a safe landing. We want to comfortably rest on placid waters, amidst skies, fanned by balmy breezes. But, we are called to bitter trials. In patience we can face life's challenges. We can walk pleasant paths and match the greatest mountains.

Patience means waiting. How do we wait? Waiting is not an empty absence of action. It is a hesitation, a pause for power, a sweeping of the skies to see that which awaits us from on high. Patience means waiting while standing still, believing that our strength will come, especially when we are passing through hard places.

Patience is not a do-nothing policy.
We wait patiently while we work for what we want to see brought to pass.
We need to drain our desires in prayer and dedicate them in labor.
We must keep on working until the day is done and the battles
of life have passed. "For we shall reap if we faint not."
There is no other way. Be Patient.

Have Patience

The word patience has always bothered me. Those of us who came along in advance of our civil rights movement remember how we were told when the slightest murmurings of protest representations were made, "Be patient." So, that word patience has always troubled me. I wanted to find out from where it came. Now, there are forms of patience that I do not take to be referred to here. There is the patience of the slave who prostrates himself or herself before the master. That is not the patience I am talking about. When the scriptures tell us to be patient, they are not talking about dumb submission, surrender, and resignation. The word patience has been misused. People of faith are not called on quietly and calmly and meekly to submit to everything.

✢

Jesus Christ never backed up. Great obstacles loomed before his pathway. He kept going forward. Mighty enemies sought to block His ministry and light. He faced them one by one and said, "I must go on today and tomorrow. There's trouble ahead, but I must go on. There is a judgment hall waiting for me, but I must go on. There is a bitter cup from which I must drink, but I must go on. . . ." Unbowed,

His shoulders back, He marched on into the storm and through the storm into the morning of endless life. That is the patience of which I speak.

✢

Why should we have anxiety about anything? Oh, we have our many desires and ambitions. We do our best, for there is no desire that comes true until we are throwing our might and main into what we seek. We may take the path of resentment, frustration, and peace-robbing puzzlement, wondering why things don't work out. Or, we can resist the urge to have our minds torn and tortured.

Patience does not work in a vacuum.
It does not function in a life that is not turned toward God.
God's promises are open to every person. Don't be anxious.
Because of your faith, you can trust in the goodness of God above.

Have Patience

In that trust, anxiety vanishes; care flees as clouds before the sunshine. What a great sense of freedom we have in turning over all of our cares and concerns to God. This is the person who says, "I will take all God wants me to have and I will be calm when God holds back from me." We have a peace that as we travel the seas of life, we have the greatest captain who ever sailed.

Remember the words of faith: "Tribulation worketh patience, and patience experience, and experience hope." Exercising patience while enduring life's challenges is difficult. We will endure suffering, experience hardship, and observe our mistakes nailed to signposts. The mere show of weakness may become the talk of the town. Do well in suffering. Take these events of life one step further. Suffer and take it patiently. Trust that this is acceptable to the One who is above.

✣

Go On! In every moment of life, among enemies and foes, exercise patience. We are not promised that if we are patient in trials that our thorny paths will turn to rose-strewn roads. We are promised that if we do so, God will be pleased by our actions. There may be no praise by men, but we will have a blessing from above. Patience in tribulations will allow us to please God.

✣

To keep courage is to believe against sight. To not give up in spirit is not idleness. It is a struggle of the first magnitude. It is not an idleness to keep hope alive. It is a job for a hero. Stand still in the spirit! That is patience—acting, praying, and laboring steadiness.

✣

A person can be patient when he knows something has a secret. The faithful can be patient because they are in possession of the secret. "For in the time of trouble God shall hide me in His pavilion. In the secret of God's tabernacle shall He hide me; God shall set me on a rock." A person possessing such a secret can say, "Wait on the Lord, be of good courage, and God shall strengthen thine heart. Wait, I say, on the Lord." With such a secret, we can hold on and hold out until the end, patient and calm. With such a secret, you can bear a little longer that old problem in your home, that irritation on your job, and carry that burden a little while longer: You've got a secret!

"In faith, possess your souls!" It is hard to suffer when we are guilty; it is doubly torturous to suffer for things we have not done. It is painful to be caught in evil doings; it is heartrending to be misunderstood when our purposes are good, our motives pure. It is troubling to be suspected when we are guilty; it is a burden grievous to be borne. Indeed, when we are suspected while trying to render a faithful account of our stewardship, what shall we do? We ask our Lord when we are innocent, but delivered up to the fiery trials of the soul. His answer is, "In your patience, possess your souls!"

☩

This patience of God is not a kind of dull resignation, a heavy-hearted acceptance of what cannot be helped. It has a rainbow in the cloud because God is in it. We chafe in our impatience with the question of when. Like the slain crying from beneath the altar, "How long, O Lord, how long?" God will not lay on us more than we can bear. "Weeping may endure for the night, but joy cometh in the morning." Yet will we praise God for God's great deliverance. "How long?" we ask. God's answer comes back, "Until all things are ready." But not until the fullness of time, when all things are ready, God will deliver.

✣

God wants us to keep God's "word of patience." That means we should take God seriously. Our problem so often is that we do not take God seriously. I am not now talking about those knee-jerk prayers we blurt out in desperation. I am talking about allowing the spirit of the Lord to permeate, to saturate, to fill us not in what we say from time to time, but in our waking thoughts and in our actions.

✣

Have Patience

Dr. W. H. Jernagin from Washington, DC, a sage of faith, told me that after eighty years of life, he learned whenever anything bad happens to him, he gets on edge, peering, scanning the horizon, looking for the good things that are sure to come. Whenever a cloud, look for the showers of blessings! Whenever a steep road, look then for the mountain-pure air and the breathtaking view. Whenever there is a heavy load to carry, look for precious strength won from bearing the load. Dr. Jernagin said, "Possess your soul, Preacher, Possess your soul!"

Hold on, even when it seems as if nothing is going to happen. So one prayer, one struggle, one effort and then another—nothing happens. But keep praying. Keep hoping, keep serving, one more effort, and one more day like all the rest. One more sacrifice like all the rest and we shall waken satisfied and in God's likeness. Hold on, work on, pray on, believe on, and trust on, and God will make it well. Be patient!

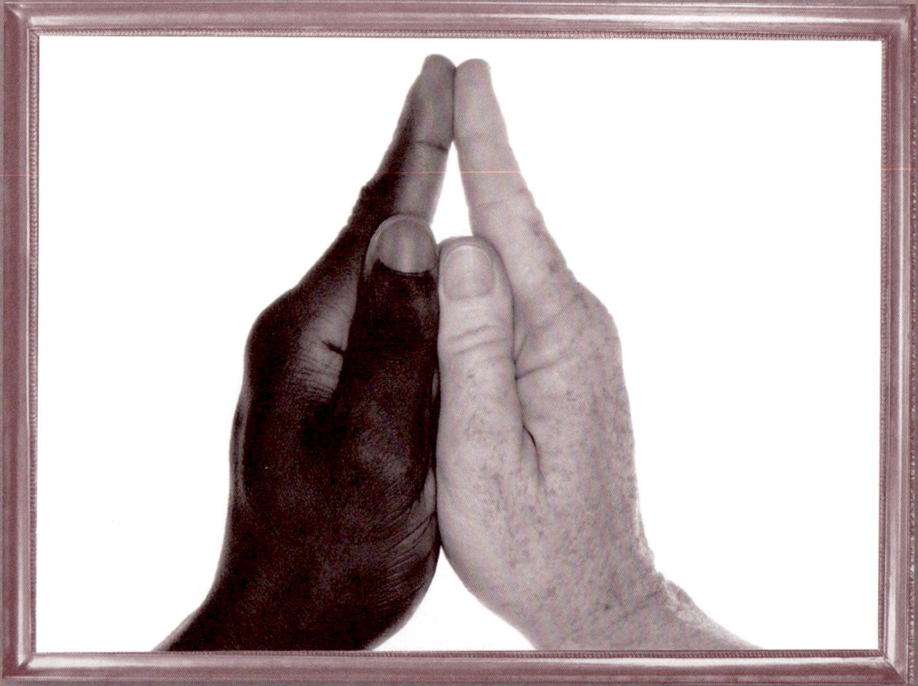

CHAPTER EIGHT

THE MATTER OF RACE

When one thinks of the emancipation of American slaves, it does seem that a right cause so surrounded by self-seekers and destructive souls would perish in the struggle. I never cease to marvel that emancipation should have come to this nation. When I add the historical figures on the side of slavery continuing, and add the historical figures on the side of slavery ending, I am convinced that the emancipation of the black slave in America was an historical impossibility. Indeed, freedom had the larger figures, but only because we forgot to add one rather large figure: the presence of a higher power who does not tire in the august purposes of Truth, Right, and Freedom. Centuries may grind by, but those purposes go on never beaten, never worn out, never dying, never ending! Race defines America underneath everything else. However, there is great sorrow these days in the hearts of many Americans who love this land and who believe that God has for it some worthier destiny than our bitter divisions of race and region.

✣

Race hate is an old and persistent disease in the bloodstream of society. Race hate is not a one-way street. This is the ultimate danger in any sin and makes race hate eligible for consideration and concern by the church. The basis of the ancient rift had been religious but was also compounded with difference of race. Even then we must say that force and thrust were in His words of wisdom and insight, but race hatred blinds us to that wisdom and insight. People of faith must press for laws that restrain the wild, primitive, savage lunges of race hatred and bigotry.

✣

We lament and wonder what our society is coming to and where those of a minority race are going to end up. Most of us who lament present conditions of crime, low achievement, low aspiration, and community indifference are comparing the admittedly frightening conditions of these days with an earlier time when people were polite to each other, when schools taught and churches were spiritually important in society, and society seemed safe and people felt secure in the streets. Those were also the times of discrimination based on race and class. Stores, downtown stores, and unions often barred minorities from employment and membership, respectively. Our Faith was born in the midst of a world in turmoil. Its noblest days have been in seasons of distress and grief. Those who live today can harvest the fruit of that faith.

Minority people must begin to raise questions as to what we can do to help ourselves. We have a deep sickness in our communities. We must find a way to get at it. Our public behavior, ill-clothed men, lurid speech, and music are repulsive to all decent people. We need more reliability, morality, and care in the rearing of children. Other communities raise millions of dollars—not in churches, but in drives and appeals—for work among youth, aged, and handicapped. We, too, can do the same.

There ought not to be a few people beleaguering the government about better education for African Americans and Latinos. Every minority parent whose child is in public schools and who is being butchered by the evils of poor education in our nation ought to bombard boards of education and government until this matter becomes a watchword, clarion call, and categorical imperative to every public official in the land.

Truly, America's passage of civil rights legislation in the 1960s was a sign of hope. There were not mass celebrations in the streets. Many of us believed that those bills should have never been necessary. America was simply doing what it should have done from the start. Many bills were passed without implementation. True implementation then and now would light the fire of our faith and cause us to believe that our nation honestly cares about personal and social freedom. What should be demanded of every person is to show justice to friend and foe, justice to self, and justice to Almighty God.

A Matter of Race

Someday some critics and latter-day deliverers who scoff and sneer at the faith of many of minority descent are going to realize that we have come this far by our faith. By faith, we have been given a sense of dignity, destiny, and hope. In another day, we had no banks, no stores, no factories, no legislators, where we could feel at home, that we mattered. But, we did have our faith. We have come this far by our faith.

✣

We must challenge this strange spectacle of shortsighted peoples, supposed leaders from different parts of the country that are not willing to close the remaining gap between whites and African Americans. There must be no first-class and second-class citizens. As a nation, we must all demand first-class citizenship for every person in our nation. I refuse to believe that God was any less at God's best when God made white people than when he made African Americans.

✣

Some time ago, a city official said to me that very sincere people in our schools do not believe that teachers with full training and experience should be directed to serve in schools in our difficult areas. Indeed, there are problems, but, regardless of race, we must endeavor to bring quality education to every person in our communities. Truly, we must stop making excuses. Society must honor the justice, fairness, and decency. Leaders must stop trying to defeat democracy's avowed purposes and support and encourage the fulfillment of those purposes.

✢

Are we to feel that our nation is about as democratic, just, and free of prejudice as most Americans want it to be? When all the deploring about discrimination is over, when all of the head-wagging and tongue-clucking in sorrow about the poor state of minority peoples are finished and done, most people in the American society are more or less satisfied with our semi-democracy. What a people determined and dedicated could do to very quickly change the outlook and image of our nation!

A Matter of Race

Thank God the Supreme Court has decided that the exclusionary practice of attorneys barring people from juries on the basis of race can no longer be done. You get the situation where blacks cannot convict blacks and whites will not convict whites. . . . And so, race has once again come to the fore to threaten our entire system of justice, which we knew was suspect all along but which now is placarded and emblazoned before the world.

✥

We are beginning to recognize that the problem of race sorely vexes our religious witness as it does our world's peace. There was a day when people boldly proclaimed the superiority of race, even supported it by spurious interpretation of scripture, a reflection on the integrity of God and the justice of the Eternal. No doctrine of race can be made to fit in the frame of the religion. We shall be people of faith at the point of race or be forced to confess we are not people of faith at all.

> *People of faith must never rush off from the hard facts of life. It is our place in all the affairs of human beings to bring them unto justice. It should not be that we are too far removed from participation in community life to ignore what is going on around us. Let it never be said that these affairs do not matter. We should bring our influence in these matters to bear with all the Spirit that is within us. The matter of race relations is our business! Liberty of conscience, worship, and equality are all marks of our faith.*

Certain regions of our own land reflect sharply the pride of race, the arrogance of color, and the unseemly emphasis on national origin, which in varying degrees afflict all of our land, to the detriment of our evangelism, both nationwide and worldwide. I am persuaded that thousands of people across this land bow in deep humiliation and in profound sorrow at their failures, at the point of class and race, to live out the glorious provision of the Evangel of Grace, which has been committed to our hands.

There is something else to be said today about our present position on race. Notwithstanding our enthusiasm and determination during the late 1960s and 1970s to right a long-standing and wrong preoccupation with race and all of the implications of race, we have come now upon a day when America apparently has grown weary of the struggle.

African Americans and whites together should take on the responsibilities of freedom. Let us give service in protest. Speaking, writing our congressmen, volunteering in civil rights organizations. There are endless creative possibilities. Go, find your place, work, and bring words of life.

In matters of race, we celebrate and encourage the young people of our country as they take up the cause of civil rights. Let God be praised for every muffled cry in slavery's dark hours that produced the proud courage of our young people. Let God be praised for every silent resentment to indignity that our forefathers registered when they could not speak and which lives in our young heroes and heroines. May freedom's muted sigh and liberty's muffled roar become a thunder and a crashing crescendo!

✣

One preacher said, I do not know the technical term, but it is puzzling to me how 50 percent of white blood, so to speak, does not make one white but 5 percent of black blood makes one black. Is there some difference in strength, or is this a matter of custom or deep prejudice? I do not know.

✣

I heard a Jewish leader of my community remind us again, not long ago and rightly, that in Hitler's Germany, race prejudice destroyed the physical lives of six million Jews, while the rest of the world scarcely raised a finger of protest. Race, the generation chasm, class antagonism . . . We continue to think of race in small, selfish terms of color or class or section, rather than in the broad terms of humanity and that sonship which is the birthright of all people.

A Matter of Race

Let us remember with honor those who paved the way for the freedoms we enjoy today: freedom riders; civil rights crusaders who marched and sat at lunch counters, those who were beaten, jailed, killed, and who battled in our nation's courts. On their shoulders rests the foundation of modern civil rights liberties. Among those who led the movement are those who were my warmest friends. I knew of their humility, gentleness of soul, and modesty of spirit. They followed the best of the American creed rather than any voice of expediency or postponement of truth. The community for which they suffered remembers them with deep affection for the redemption of a nation from the shame of segregation.

FAITH IN THE FIRE

Martin Luther King, Jr., was legend in lands far beyond the sea, to say nothing of America. He came among the thorny problems of the land armed with a massive mind, prophetic insight, and a soul sensitized in the group sorrow of the South. He came to the hour in America's history endowed with a total dedication to democracy's brightest dreams and with freedom's fire leaping from his heart and out of his mouth like molten lava from a seething crater. As the nation reckons its heroes with unbiased eyes, it counts itself glad that King is among its sons and that the pilgrimage of the republic to the city of truth and freedom . . . he would not spare it, would not allow it to cravenly quit at some halfway house, too ignoble for its destiny and too cramped for the amplitude of its role in history.

A Matter of Race

All too often our political campaigns degenerate into exploitation of what is ignoble in the American makeup; manufacturing villains, creating enemies, courting old fears and resentments of race, color, section, and class. Our civil rights leaders must not engage in yeoman service. Many have pathetically miscalculated the dimensions of this present election year. Each must understand the depth and breadth of what America faces during this fateful election year. African Americans must realize that the outcome of this election [2008] is far beyond a matter of civil rights. The United States of America is on trial.

☩

Victor Hugo commented once that "there is nothing so irresistible as an idea whose time has come." Likewise, in America freedom's hour has struck. America has come to a new path. Whether in the bondage and chafe in chains, a great stirring is occurring. Freedom's morning has come. The earth's children are looking anxiously for deliverance. America is leading the way. Let America be the example for the peoples of the world; may the bell of our republic ring as we continue to develop into the fullness of what the founders of our nation promised.

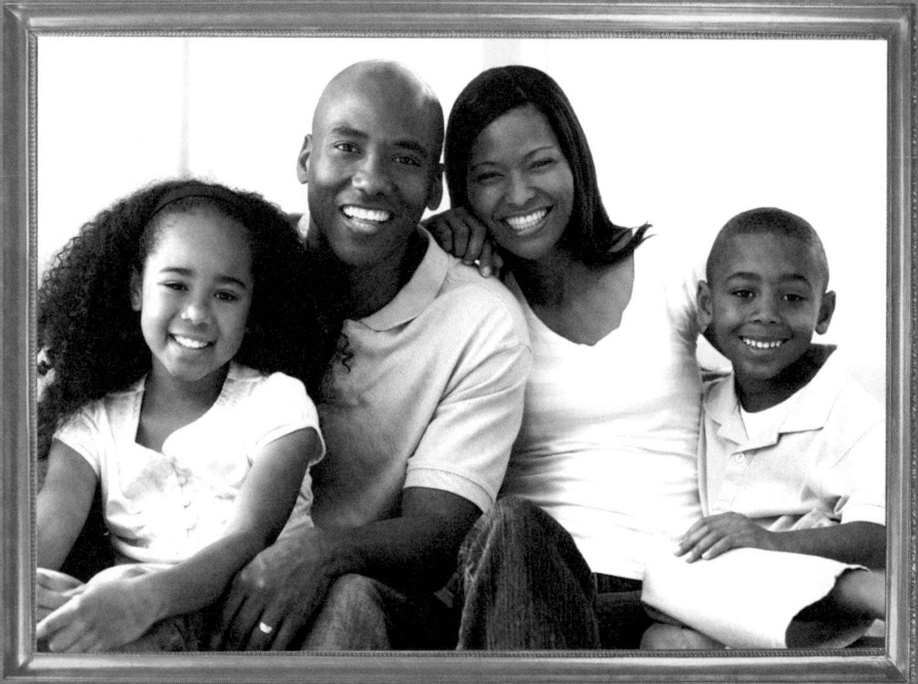

CHAPTER NINE

IT'S ALL IN THE FAMILY

We are understandably alarmed these days by the harvest we are reaping from the loss of the family. The family relationship is, in all likelihood, the pivotal human contract; historians and sociologists telling us that the history of the human race reveals no time when the family unit was not. In many respects, it appears that we are too much of so many unnecessary things, too shrewd to be believers, too busy to be worshippers, too busy to show respect for others, too sophisticated to practice simple family virtues of scriptural reading, family prayer.

✥

We need family. God never did anything kinder for our psychological and physical development than when the arrangement was made in the genes and makeups of our parents that they would take an interest in us and see about us.

Many families believed that salvation lay in the great cities of our country. Some thought them to be heaven itself. A generation whose sight never got up above the sight of the great buildings couldn't become anything except savages, substituting homemade guns for spears, gangs for the tribe, with bloodletting as the only thrilling game they can play. Whenever we lose sight of those things spiritual, whenever the family fails to keep alive the presence of our neighbor God, savagery is the natural conclusion. Only the home and family can change this direction.

It's All in the Family

The weakness of family life is too prevalent among us. The incidence of broken homes is all too many; the number of illegitimate births is all too high. We owe our children something better than they are being given in this community. No community which is to grow and thrive can allow any other community to degrade it or deny it to the point where it collapses and abandons its determination to give each succeeding generation a little more of hope and dignity.

✢

We are being called into a new time and way in our families. Our young men and women must be trained and taught to see women with a new regard and a new sense of responsibility. The filthy language, which is spoken on our streets, degrades us, but when it is tossed about in the harming of women, both young and elder, it becomes a measureless shame and a disgrace. The sanctity of womanhood must become a reality with us if we are going to make it.

Our children often grow away from us. How painful it is to realize our children grow away from us, asserting independence from our wisdom and wishes. However deep the wounds and anxieties of these experiences, our children's growth and self-determination speak to our love, care, and concern we invested in them. The end of this delicate dependence speaks to the setting of the course to which their lives must steer. The greatest example of this is marriage. In that union, our children become who they're meant to be and step out on the foundation we have provided for them. It is our continuing prayer that the voices of their past and the voice of the Eternal attend and order the steps of their new life. There is perhaps no joy to match that of harmonious love in family where two generations are able to live not only in peace, but also in love.

✣

In family affairs, life is a strange mixture of joy and sorrow. There are times when we laugh and those all too frequent hours when we must weep. What is harder to bear is the long, seemingly endless, gray, and dull day when there is neither sunshine nor rain. Family life consists of both happiness and sadness. The purpose of our family is found in both. There are splendid people, honorable, charitable, whose love we bear in life and in death, who seem to have something missing in their lives: radiance, a sense of glad peace, and a purpose.

✧

Is your family falling to pieces because you cannot admit a mistake? We can all understand and appreciate the plight of a family, which exists in a set of circumstances less than ideal. Happy and healthy are families, which seek quiet time together. Time around the family table—there is a oneness and wholeness, gladness in their family closeness.

✧

How sad it is to see any young people miss out on life's successes and life's rewards. It is even sadder to see one who has thrown away every golden opportunity, who has trifled away the precious few years of youth when preparation for life is at its normal and best advantage. How sad to see them scuffling and straining later, trying to regain lost ground, neglected opportunity. Sadder still is to see someone who fails to use his or her every chance, parents willing to sacrifice, schools wide open, churches eager, a variety of professions and opportunities available. The time comes when such is no more and whatever that person has become or failed is forever true.

In the much closer geographical context of family life, our physical comforts are beyond the wildest imaginings of earlier generations. Think of the comforts and conveniences in your own family. Our family ties are crucial. We who do not know such strong ties of family will find it hard to appreciate what spiritual sacrifices have been made on our behalf.

It's All in the Family

Perhaps our families are collapsing around us. In a sense, we may personally feel our families are at the breaking point. We part from scenes of childhood, from our family, our roots, from our first friends. The passing of many years has not erased from memory a particular evening of homesickness at being ten thousand miles from home and family, which came over me like a physical ache. The time of evening was that strangely touching hour when day turns quietly to night and all of the family has come from here and there to gather in the light and warmth and joy of home. I looked at such a house, a lamp burning in what I took to be the living room with family gathered there. It was not my family or my home, and the door was closed to me.

※

Among the choicest actions ever executed by a person is when love and friendship bind young and elder together. In old age and childlessness, in travel, and commitment, each ties their hearts to one another. The words exchanged here are breathless, touching, heartrending words. The sentiment abides in the absence of others, prosperity and support.

Every day we enshrine our blessed parents with the enduring monuments of our own improved character. Our celebration of their lives assumes its worthiest proportions and our lives are ever drawn closer to their spirits. Perhaps chief among these memories are the thoughts, which recounted over and over like a cathedral bell, of our parents' voices praying for us; a power their experience taught them to be able to tame the tigers and to give power to the faint. Their knowledge of the ways of the world may have seemed so limited and so inadequate and yet out of their experience they threw the promise that they would pray for us against any odds and disasters and temptations that may come upon us. Those prayers have steered children toward peaceful ways and a loving world.

☦

As parents rear their children, who knows what blessing of womanhood or manhood will come of these little babies. Might not one of them become the means by which humanity's long, cruel ways of war are changed, and a new era of peace and liberty comes to the sons of men everywhere? Which one of them might turn out to be the means by which gates of new life are open to countless numbers?

It's All in the Family

The parents of the world are proof positive that there are loyalties in us more powerful than our own comfort. The mothers of the world prove that humanity has in it the capacity to take risks for something better than mere cause and painlessness. Something from heaven is breathed into our mothers and fathers who, against all odds, cling to, in the face of contrary evidence, that things will get better for their children. Even in a society that slams doors in the face of some, those who rear us believe that their child will find opportunity. This is the hero in our parents, a heroism that confounds and refutes all the critics of the human soul and detractors of the spirit of humankind.

FAITH IN THE FIRE

―――――――――――――

We should all thank the heavens for the faith of our parents, for so sweet a spirit, so humble in success, so trusting in faith, so kind in disposition, so helpful in manner, so fervent in prayer, so forgiving in heart, so long-suffering in trouble, and so steadfast in storms of life.

―――――――――――――

One of the greatest tragedies which can happen to any people or any family is that of reduction of the status of the father symbol, for God has given fathers in order that we might know the meaning of firmness mixed with tenderness, and mothers that we might know tenderness mixed with firmness.

✧

We often have tearful reflections on the sweetness of our parents; when we consider how we have benefited from great sacrifices, which our mothers and fathers have made. What wonderful thoughts are thinking of kindness, love, and protection, which you received from the loving and caring hands and heart? It was because of them that I have been given a chance. Not one of us ever makes it unless someone gives us our chance. For those who have known such love, care, and interest, it is easy to remember and feel gladness mingled with sorrow.

✢

Parents who are God-fearing people are often called on to suffer great sorrow because of their children. Thoughtless husbands cause innocent wives a Gethsemane of heartbreaks. Willful, foolish wives hang like millstones around the necks of well-meaning, unoffending husbands. Children are called upon to endure great trials and to be scarred by the mistakes of their parents. We are witnessing a tragic example of such happenings today. The upheaval, agony, and blind lunging which occur are seeds sown in America's past and cultivated as a crop found in fields of anger, brutality, and shame.

We are thankful for homes where prayer is no stranger. We are thankful for homes where human ingenuity ran out, and mothers and fathers did not know what the next step would be, but believed some one provision would come. We are thankful for the drying hands of parents for children's tears and homes in which faith abides.

✣ ✣ ✣

LeRoy Henderson

CHAPTER TEN

EVERYDAY WIT

*I*n the Great Depression of 1929, the federal government, under the leadership of President Franklin Roosevelt, arranged for farm agents to go throughout the South advising farmers how they could improve their methods and save money and make better crops. This was done in Louisiana. One farm agent visiting a farmer asked him to come to a meeting. "Why should I? What is to occur at the meeting?" said the farmer. "Oh, we are going to show you how to do better with your farming and raise more crops." "Oh," said the farmer, "I don't need to come. I'm not doing all I know to do now."

Some of Woodrow Wilson's cabinet was hunting in Virginia and they came to a posted fence that said "No Trespassing." They then went on in unabashed. There was a black caretaker of the farm and he said to them when they came in, "You can't hunt here. This is posted land. No trespassing." So one of the cabinet members said, "You do not recognize that this is Mr. Cameron who is secretary of war in the cabinet of Woodrow Wilson?" The caretaker said, "I don't care if he is Booker T. Washington. He can't hunt here."

Alexander White was a preacher of severe righteousness and damnation at St. George's on Princes Street in Edinburgh. Hugh Black came to be his assistant, and White preached in the morning and Black preached in the evening. It was said that White blackened the saints in the morning and Black whitewashed the sinners at night.

Seventy years ago, at the Louisiana Baptist State Convention, there was a secretary. He was criticized once for getting more income and being honored with gratuities more than others, and the attackers said it was a matter of "big fish eating the little fish," to which the secretary replied, "What do you expect the big fish to eat but the little fish?"

⁕

Dr. E. W. Perry used to tell of two vagrants sitting on a park bench in downtown Oklahoma City, and one looking up at a tall skyscraper and saying to the other, "I came within one word of owning that building." "Oh, how?" said the other. "Well, I asked the owner to give it to me." "What did he say?" "He said 'no,' but suppose he had said 'yes.'"

⁕

Three ministers were under consideration for the pastorate of a certain church. One was to preach at 11:00 A.M., the other was to preach at 3:00 in the afternoon, and the third was to preach at 7:30 in the evening. That morning, the first preacher took his text from the 21st chapter of the Gospel of John and the third verse. He took his text from the first part of that verse: "Simon Peter saith unto them, I go fishing." The second preacher, preaching at 3:00 in the afternoon, used the same text: "They say unto him, 'We also go with thee.'" The third preacher at 7:30 that evening thought to use the same verse, for whatever reason, and that portion of the verse which says, "They went forth, and entered into a ship immediately; and that night they caught nothing."

✢

Dr. William Carrington, who was pastor for a long time of the First A.M.E. Zion Church in Brooklyn and who should have, given his eloquence and his integrity, been elected bishop but never was, used to tell of a man in a church, I think that he pastored in North Carolina. "This church needs to be painted," he said. "If I had the money and if I had the wherewithal, I would have it painted myself." He said this over and over again, "This church needs painting. If I had the means and wherewithal, I would have it painted by myself." Finally, a relative died and a fraternal organization left a policy to this gentleman: several hundred dollars. People waited, and the man did not ever say when he was going to have the church painted. Finally, the committee went to see him and he said, "Well, I'll tell you the truth. When I had the will, I didn't have the wherewithal, but when I got the wherewithal, I lost the will."

✣

In the early 1940s, there were two preachers in New Orleans who were very given to extraordinary, extensive, expansive accounts of what they were doing. They were supposed to be very prominent in the political order of New Orleans at a time when blacks were not allowed to vote. Once, one of them, Morgan, said to Curtis, "You know, Mayor Maestri, who was the mayor of New Orleans, has asked me to go out into the river parishes and out into the country parishes to get some support for the next campaign, and he is going to grant me $8,000 or $9,000." And Curtis said, "Wait a minute, Morgan. We tell other people that. This is Curtis you are talking to. You know, we talk the same talk." And then Morgan said, "Oh, excuse me, Curtis, I forgot."

✣

When I had been pastor for 20-odd years, I made a comment half in jest one evening at a celebration for my 22nd or 23rd anniversary that I had been preceded in the Concord Church by four pastors over 110 years, and that meant that each pastor had served almost 20-odd years and died there. I said quite jokingly that evening that the truth is, "This church does not know how to get rid of a pastor, to put a pastor out." One of my dearest friends, Deacon Cyprian Belle, long gone now, said to me, laughing, "We know how." And we always laughed about it.

Mr. Jim Rhodes was a porter on the L and A, the Louisiana and Arkansas Railroad, which ran between Shreveport and Baton Rouge when I was a lad. Mr. Rhodes used to say that I was Baptist-born and Baptist-bred, and when I die, it will be Baptist-dead.

C. T. Walker of the Tabernacle Church in Augusta would have been received as the finest preacher of color in a generation. Walker died in 1921, or there about. He was buried right alongside the church. His tomb is still there. One of his successors was Charles Hamilton who had been a professor at Morehouse College School of Religion. My dear friend in Brooklyn, William Jones of Bethany Baptist Church, asked Hamilton how long did Walker pastor at Tabernacle Church? Ruefully, Hamilton said, "He's still pastoring."

✢

My uncle Manny had a gift for saying things simply. He said, "Money will not make you happy, but you can be so comfortable while unhappy if you got it."

✢

My colleague, Sandy Ray, and I were driving together to Buffalo to get to Niagara Falls, and we stopped and asked a gentleman the way to the falls. He said, "I could send you down by Route 15, but I won't do that. I could send you down also to the falls by taking 17, but I don't think I'll do that." Dr. Ray said, "Drive on, Gardner. This man is telling us many ways not to get there, but he hasn't given us one way to get there."

The preacher who deals with the text without knowing the context of the text is likely to end up with a pretext, stating some prejudice of his.

If the minister thinks poorly of his people, his people are sure to think unfavorably of him.

☩

Tom Phillips, pastor in Morgan City, Louisiana said that the Baptist Church must be the church of Jesus Christ, because it could not have survived with all of the missteps and the foolishness and the strange ways it has adopted.

✢

In the 1920s and the very earliest 1930s, L. K. Williams was the esteemed pastor of the Olivet Baptist Church in Chicago, reputed to be the largest Baptist church among people of color. He was also president of the National Baptist Convention. At any rate, a man was elected to the board of deacons at the church. At the next deacon meeting Dr. Williams made some proposal that the church ought to do. This deacon rose and said, "I don't know, Dr. Williams. I'm not prepared to agree with that until I get more explanation. In fact, I am opposed to what you have said." Quickly Dr. Williams's idea passed. At the next meeting, Steve Griffin, who was chairman of the Board of Deacons, was there when this new deacon arrived. He said to the new deacon, "You know, you're not a member of the deacon board anymore." "Well, why," said the man. "I was just elected at the meeting before last, and I have just been to one meeting." Griffin replied, "Do you remember when you raised that question about what Dr. Williams said?" "Yes, I remember that." "Well, that was the moment you left the board of deacons."

George Buttrick, pastor of Madison Avenue Presbyterian Church in New York, was in conversation with Norman Vincent Peale, the true father of the modern version of self-improvement and prosperity through religion. Peale had written often about "the inferiority complex." Buttrick said, "Norman, if a person has an inferiority complex, might it be because he is inferior?"

I belong to the Christian Faith Baptist Church, pastored and founded by Dr. David Forbes, and which was once visited to the great delight of all the people by Tavis Smiley and Cornel West. There appeared in the church's paper some comments on that Sunday that I think bear repeating. First: Why pay for a GPS? Jesus steers our direction for free. Second: Jesus died for my space in heaven. Third: Where will you spend eternity, smoking or non-smoking? Fourth: God so loved the world that He did not send a committee. Fifth: God sends no one away empty except those who are full of themselves.

Alan Greenspan, the former Federal Reserve chairman, in what sounds almost like an excerpt from a sermon, has said, "Unless somebody can find a way to change human nature, we will have more crises."

※

D. Ward Nichols was bishop in the African Methodist church for many years, and he said that when one of his Harlem churches became vacant by death, the officers of the church came to him and said, "We do not want a bishop, and for our church to be put in mourning forever." He did not first catch what they meant. He later found out they did not want a preacher of dark complexion. Bishop Nichols said when he realized what they meant, he said to them, "Richard Hilderbrand, a preacher of unmistakable ebony hue with remarkable gifts." Richard Hilderbrand later became a bishop.

I was really honored to be pastor of the Concord Baptist Church in Brooklyn for 42 years. Among my earliest predecessors were one who bore the name of Sampson White and another Leonard Black, so that our church was established on the Black and the White.

✣

In 1961, a bittersweet memory: the National Baptist Convention meeting in Kansas City was having a contest for the presidency of the convention. Dr. J. H. Jackson of Chicago was the incumbent. I was the aspirant. Now, Dr. Billups was head of the Louisiana Baptist Convention and had been a great friend and colleague of mine, and really had been a protégé of my father, Washington Monroe Taylor. At any rate, Dr. Billups, who was a Jackson supporter, said, "All of those who support Dr. Jackson will go over here," meaning to one side of the room. And when they had stood, one lone man asked, "Where are the people who are supporting Taylor to go?" To which Dr. Billups said, "They can go to hell."

✣

Roscoe Conkling Simmons was one of the most celebrated black orators of his generation and was given to a great deal of self-confidence. He once said that he was in London and a presiding officer said, "Mr. Roscoe Conkling Simmons will speak to us." "Aye," said Simmons. "How long should I speak?" The presiding officer said, "Speak as long as you wish, Mr. Simmons." And then, Roscoe Conkling Simmons said, "I spoke all night."

A preacher had reached his peroration.
He was expounding and saying that,
"If the Lord be for you, who can be against you?"
And he repeated it two times, "Who can be against you?"
From the middle of the small church, one man apparently
not in love with the pastor said, "The people, man, the people."

While reading from his manuscript years ago, the preacher mixed the pages and finally said to the people, "I've lost my way right now, but I am on my way to Zion."

A speaker being introduced to a sparse audience received an apology for the size of the audience, to which he replied that the Lord Jehovah did not mind speaking to one man, Moses, on the mountain. What size audience did he, the speaker, need?

A speaker I know received at the beginning of his speech, a statement, a standing ovation from the audience, to which he replied, "I am surprised and a little disappointed to find that you will stand for anything."

Adolph Wiggins said that a woman in Baton Rouge in the 1920s was seen rushing to a church. A neighbor asked her, "Where are you going?" She said, "I am going to a funeral." "Oh," said the neighbor. "Who is dead?" "I don't know," she said. "But Wash Taylor is preaching." That was my father. Adolph Wiggins used to tell that 46 years ago in our town.

✢

In Baton Rouge where I grew up, my father was pastor in the 1920s of the Mount Zion Baptist Church. Mrs. Rosa Hampton, a long time member, explained why she did not attend an important meeting. "I was tired," she said. Mr. Andrew Holman, deacon, said, "The good Lord promised us rest on the other side of the river, not on this side." There is no record of what Mrs. Hampton said after that.

✢

In Baton Rouge, Dave Lewis used to say, "Many start but few go. Many think but few know."

It is said that if someone needs an introduction, he does not deserve it, and if he deserves an introduction, he does not need it.

✢

During a much more oppressive time for blacks, the superintendent (white, of course) of the Parish School Board, having promised the black principal over and over again a new school for black children who had been meeting for generations in the church, finally said, "George, I won't be able to keep that promise. I won't be able to build a school for the black children. We have to build another school for the education of our white children," to which the black principal said, "Oh, that's all right, Mr. Hatcher. There's nothing our white children need like education."

✢

Many years ago, there was a popular song, "Have You Ever Seen a Dream Walking," which Professor Lagrand—as we called high school teachers back then—upon hearing the young people at McKinley High School singing that, said, "I haven't seen a dream walking, but I've seen, when I look at you young people, many nightmares walking."

---

*My wife, Phillis Strong, grew up in a home to which
W. E. B. Du Bois was a close friend and often a guest at their home.
I have argued with her that Booker Washington left the great institution
Tuskegee, but Dr. Du Bois left no institution of the kind like Tuskegee,
but she always counters with the argument that he left an idea.
An idea with a quality of high destiny. And he wrote books for
black people and for the world's blacks, pointing to a bright future,
which may be, in a way of speaking,
more powerful than an institution.*

In my childhood 80 years ago, there was a man who passed my mother's house with some regularity whose name was Mr. Deemer Bell. He was a member of one of the secret orders that proliferated in that day in my native state of Louisiana. He would pass my mother's house. I would run to him, having learned something about these secret orders and ask, "Mr. Bell, what is the password?" And he would with great ceremony lean over and whisper in my ear, "Be good." Thank you, Mr. Bell. I have never forgotten that in 80 years.

✧

Mr. Joe Williams was a great friend of my family. Mr. Joe could neither read nor write but he would ask me often about something in the paper or whatnot. "Garden [he never called me Gardner], what do it say?" And I would tell him. But Mr. Joe, unable to read or write, somehow bought a nice house in Baton Rouge and when he died he left it to me. I have never forgotten that.

✧

Apparently, Mrs. Mary Todd Lincoln was a constant critic and faultfinder with President Lincoln, his ways, and his speech, although she loved him very dearly. Finally, one cabinet member said, "Mr. President, I don't see how you stand the constant badgering of Mrs. Lincoln, if you don't mind my saying so. I marvel that you take it as well as you do." Mr. Lincoln replied, "Well, Mary's criticisms seem to do her a lot of good and they do me no harm."

✢

A devout lady went to church hungering for the Gospel. When she came home, she said to someone who had not gone, "I was hungry for the Gospel, but the preacher took so long setting the table that I lost my appetite."

✢

Cardinal Wolsey helped Henry VIII in more than one divorce, and in violation of his Roman Catholic oath about divorce. Finally, Henry became displeased with Wolsey and had him confined to the London Tower. Shakespeare has put on Wolsey's lips the words, "If I had served my God with half the zeal I have served my king, He would not leave me naked in my old age."

It is unquestionable that the poorest preacher may be taught to be a better preacher. The better preacher may become a good preacher. Beyond that, excellence may be impossible.

That He is able to keep, not that we are able, is the secret of Christianity. In Matthew 7:14, Jesus said, "Straight is the gate and narrow is the way which leadeth unto life and few there be that find it." Nothing is more natural to us than to hang around, hovering around the straight gate trying to decide whether we can make it wider or make ourselves a little narrower so as to enter. But for one preacher who was rather logical, it was said that he loved expansion more than he did exactness.

Robert Livingston said many years ago, "No conviction is burned more deeply into the inner heart of the world than this, that sin has not done with us when we have done with sin. There are men and women by the hundred thousands who would gladly give all they possess if they could but lay their hands upon the one hour of madness and pluck it from the past."

"The moving finger writes, and having writ, moves on: nor all your piety nor wit shall lure it back to cancel half a line, nor all your tears wash out a word of it." (Edward Fitzgerald)

*A preacher once raised the question,
"What if this life is our exile, and captivity and death
may be our return home?"*

We human beings have an appendix, which we do not need. When it becomes infected and we have appendicitis, we do need to be without it. Many of our habits, institutions, are purposeless within, and they need to be necessarily out.

A preacher was seeking a place in one of the churches of Scotland as pastor. He was from inland Scotland, and the fishing boats in some parts of Scotland have gunwales, apertures to hold the guns in the side of the ship when it had served as a fighter craft. And this preacher in his enthusiasm asked for the fishermen when catching fish that would go over the gunwales, to which a man native to that region said, "No, man. The ship will sink if they go over the gunwales."

✢

My father, in preaching, was arguing for the necessity of following the method of entrance into our Baptist churches by confession of faith and by baptism. He said that if he was told that there was no longer any cost for crossing the Mississippi River, which runs from Baton Rouge to Port Allen and which was maybe $0.10 or $0.20 per crossing, he would rather have the $0.10 or $0.20, whatever it took to cross the river, in his hand in order to pay it, if it was needed. If it was not needed, it would not hurt him to have $0.20 in his pocket, and so he made an argument for anyone to enter the faith by the regular means of confession and baptism.

☦

A young aspirant for the ministry was being examined as to his understanding of damnation and salvation. He was asked, "Would you be willing to be damned for the Gospel?" to which the ordinand replied, "Yes, sir, and I would be willing for this whole council to be damned for the same purpose."

☦

My friend, Vernon Jordan, was playing golf with President Clinton, and I had occasion to talk with the President by telephone later. I told him I heard that he had played golf with Vernon, and I asked how did the match come out. The President said, "He did not tell you how it came out?" I said no. He said, "Then, you know how it came out."

Getty Images. Photographer Michael Lutzky

CHAPTER ELEVEN

LAUGHTER IS GOOD FOR THE SOUL

When I first went to New York to pastor in 1948, my best friend until his death was Rudolph Thomas, then head of the Harlem YMCA, and executive director, whose friendship had been given to me, as so many other things in my early life were, by Marshall Shepard, who had been Recorder of Deeds, successor to Frederick Douglass who had held that position. There were very, very, very few hotels that admitted people of color in 1948. There were very few in New York; hardly any. It was said that if you sat in the lobby of the Harlem 135th Street YMCA, sooner or later you would see every black man of prominence pass through the lobby, for there was no other place to stay. Rudolph was head of all of that, and had risen from elevator boy. He knew New York as very few people did–an intimate of its political, social, religious life. I benefited from that. One of the most charming things he used to tell was of his growing up in Orlando, Florida.

His mother, as was the custom back there, baked fruitcake for Christmas in October, drenched, or sprinkled, with the appropriate liquid—whiskey; putting this under the bed so the whiskey might permeate the fruitcake, which gave it a peculiar and attractive bite. Once, a ball he was playing with on the floor rolled under the bed. He went under the bed to get his ball. He found the fruitcake while looking for the lost ball. So he pinched off the least bit of the fruitcake and found he liked the flavor. The next day in school, he said that by two o'clock in the afternoon, he could hardly think of anything except that cake, and so he would pinch off another little bit of the cake. Each afternoon that happened, day after day after day. Finally, close to December 25 came, Christmas Day, and his mother reached under the bed to get her cake and found these huge gouges out of the cake. There was not very much cake left. She said to him—she always called him Rudy—she said, "Rudolph, come here." Rudy said to himself, "Oh, Lord, Judgment Day has come."

A man lying in bed all bandaged almost from hand to foot in the hospital said to his friend, "You know I had too much to drink. You shouldn't have let me try to leap from seven stories across the street to another hotel." The other man said, "I truly am sorry, but I was so far gone with drink that I thought you could make it."

⁂

A monkey was serving as an usher and master of the seating arrangements at an animal convention. He ordered the rabbit to sit in one place and he ordered the dog to sit in another. He said, "You sit here and you sit there." Finally, the gorilla came in and asked where he should sit. And the monkey said, "Mr. Gorilla will sit anywhere he wants to sit."

⁂

When I went to New Orleans to pastor in 1941, or whatever it was I was trying to do, one of the oldest and most honorable pastors in New Orleans was named J. A. Burrell, pastor of Progressive Baptist Church, and there was a picture of him inside the church. There was a clock in what we called the vestibule, but now the Narthex. Some people wanted to honor him, so they took the clock down in the vestibule, the Narthex, and put his likeness up instead. Somebody came to church the next Sunday who apparently was not as enthusiastic about the pastor's long service, and looking at his picture in place of the clock that had been there, said, "Oh, Lord, they took down time and put up eternity."

✢

A man in the New York legislature arguing against a bill before the legislature said, "I will oppose this bill until hell freezes over and then I will oppose it on the ice."

I am a native of Louisiana. There were many secret orders around the bayous and the Mississippi River towns. Given the peculiar jumble of languages that became a part of our history—French, English, Spanish, African—our pronunciation of words sometimes strayed strangely from their original sound. The treasurer of one of those secret orders, the Knights and Ladies of Honor of America (one of those terms of compensating pride in which I grew up under the tutelage of my Aunt Gert, whom I called Ma), was giving a report of expenditures. He cited $3 for water, $2 for the sign painter, $11 for miscellany, $7 for the janitor, $8 for the chauffeur, and $13 for miscellany. Finally, one elderly member of the organization rose and asked the question, "Who is this Miss Laney who is getting all of our money?"

A pastor whom I knew long ago was elected pastor of one of our Baptist churches. He was of modest credentials, achievements, and gifts, and the church was a significant one for that community. Some of his friends said to him, "How are you going to grow into a stature that will enable you to pastor that church?" "Oh," he said, "That's no problem. If they will give me six months or a year, everything will be all right. I will cut it down to my size."

☩

A crime boss in New York was interviewing applicants for consideration to become keepers of the accounts of the syndicate. He told one accountant that he was going to have to pass a test. The accountant said, "All right," and the crime boss said, "How much is two plus two?" The accountant said, "How much do you want it to be?" The crime boss said, "You are hired."

☩

My friend Wyatt Walker, who meant so much to Dr. King's campaign, has told of an incident in Kenya in which a zebra was slow and droopy. The zebra was whining, "I'm depressed. I don't know whether I'm white with black stripes or black with white stripes." He asked the giraffe, who could not answer, and neither could a lion or an ostrich. Finally, he gave up and died and went to heaven. St. Peter noticed that the zebra, even in heaven, looked very sad. "What's wrong with you?" St. Peter asked. "I have a problem with my identity; I don't know whether I'm white with black stripes or black with white stripes. Do you know?" St. Peter said he didn't know, but that he would arrange an audience with God, who knows everything. Before long, the zebra was ushered into the door, and when God wanted to know what was wrong, the zebra repeated his complaint, "I don't know whether I'm white with black stripes or black with white stripes." God said to him, "You are what you are." The zebra returned to St. Peter, who asked, "What did God say?" The zebra reported, "God said, 'You are what you are.'" St. Peter said, "Then you are white." "How do you know?" said the zebra. St. Peter answered, "If you were black with white stripes, He would have said, 'You is what you is.'"

✢

My colleague in Brooklyn, Sandy Ray, used to tell of a time when they had started having interracial ministerial meetings in Columbus, Ohio. One preacher, who was white, said that he prepared his sermon but that it never seemed to reach home, never seemed to be of any great importance to people. People did not come to church, as he thought they ought. One of the black preachers stood up and asked him, "When do you prepare your sermons?" "Oh," said the white preacher, "I start on Monday and I work Tuesday, Wednesday, and Thursday, and by Friday I hope to have it finished." "Ah," said the black preacher, "There is your trouble. What you are doing, you are preparing and the devil is finding out what you are preparing and he is keeping your sermon to a low value. You see, I have a great number of people because when I preach, the devil does not know what I'm going to say. As a matter of fact, I don't know what I'm going to say."

✢

A man went to see his doctor for his cold, which was rather serious. He gave the doctor a check, and the doctor saw him. Later the doctor said, "You know, that check you gave me when you came to see me about your cold came back." The man said, "My cold did, too."

Laughter Is Good for the Soul

A man was making a speech. After about three or four minutes of speaking, somebody from the back shouted out, "I can't hear you." A man in the front seat said, "I can hear him. You can have my seat."

As a young pastor in Baton Rouge, Louisiana, I pastored the Mount Zion First African Baptist Church, which was supposed to be the old, established church, but I was pleased at the same time to chauffer or drive the car for the president of our state convention, Dr. T. A. Levee, who had been a great friend of my father's. We were coming at night from one of the river towns after an extra session of the convention. I was driving, Dr. Levee was sitting beside me, and we were carrying to Baton Rouge an elderly preacher named L. C. Simon. As we drove through the night, we would come to little towns; there were no superhighways. Dr. Levee was trying to nod off, but Dr. Simon would say to him, "Dr. Levee," as he called him, "What town is this?"

"I believe this is Prairieville."

"Oh. Did you know old Reverend Baylor who pastored here?"

"No," Dr. Levee said, "I don't think so."

Dr. Simon would say, "It must have been before your time."

A few miles up the road, we would come to another town, Donaldsville, and Dr. Levee was trying to sleep when Dr. Simon said, "Dr. Levee," as he called him, "Is this Donaldsville?"

"Yes, I think so," Dr. Levee would say. Dr. Simon would ask, "Did you know Reverend Bryant who pastored here years ago?"

Dr. Levee would say, "No, I don't think so." And Dr. Simon would say, "Oh, it must have been before your time."

When we came to another town, as Dr. Levee would try to fall asleep, Dr. Simon would say, "Dr. Levee, are we in White Castle?" And Dr. Levee would rouse himself and say, "I think this is Dorseyville. I think we are in Dorseyville."

"Oh, did you know Reverend Steptoe who pastored here, years ago?" And Dr. Levee would say, "No, Reverend, I don't think I did."

"Oh," Dr. Simon said. "That must have been before your time."

When we finally got to Baton Rouge, after driving through those little river towns every five or ten miles, Reverend Simon got out of the car, and Dr. Levee said to me, "Taylor, that old man got on my nerves tonight." You see, Dr. Levee was about the same age as Dr. Simon.

⁕

It must have been 1936 or 1937 when I was playing football at Leland College. The coach of my football team was named Frank Dixon. We had a young man, Albert Fontano from Alexandria, who considered himself quite an excellent running back. The coach had not put Fontano in the backfield, and so he complained, "You told me I would play in some of the game." And Coach Dixon said, "Oh, I'm saving you, Fontano." At about the end of the second half, he said, "Put me in, Coach." "No, I'm saving you." The third quarter went by and into the fourth quarter, down to about the last ten minutes, and Fontano said, "Coach, when you are going to put me in?" And Coach Dixon said, "I'm saving you for the dance tonight."

⁕

A man with obviously three or four drinks too many staggered to the ticket window at the 30th Street Station in Philadelphia and asked the ticket agent, "How much is a ticket from Philadelphia to Harrisburg?" The agent said, "That would be $3.50." "Thank you." He wandered away and turned up a few minutes later and asked the same ticket agent, "How much is a ticket from Harrisburg to Philadelphia?" The ticket agent, somewhat agitated, said, "Well, look, if it's $3.50 from Philadelphia to Harrisburg, it is $3.50 from Harrisburg to Philadelphia." "Wait a minute, my man," the customer said. "That's not necessarily so. It is not the same distance from New Year's to Christmas as it is from Christmas to New Year's."

☦

In the First District Baptist Association of which I was a member when I first finished Oberlin Graduate School, there were frequent arguments that could become very heated, and one of my elders said to the other, "I'll eat you whole," to which the other said, "If you do, you will have more sense in your belly then you have in your head."

The Spanish opera star, Placido Domingo, sang at the funeral of Senator Edward Kennedy. It reminded me of something Mr. Domingo told. He said at La Scala Opera House in Milan, one of the great opera houses of the world, he sang in a famous opera, and when he had finished the final aria, there was a pause from the audience, and then a cry rose: *"Encora, encora."* So he sang it again, and when he had finished, the same cry went up along with applause, *"Encora, encora!"* So, he sang it a third time, and when he had finished, again that same cry went up along with applause: *"Encora! Encora!"* Summoning what modesty he could, the tenor said, "How many times do you want me to sing this aria?" Many voices cried out from the orchestra and balcony, "Until you get it right!"

✢

Dwight Moody was a great American evangelist of another generation. He was carrying on a meeting in one of our large American cities, and one morning during the meeting, he asked a lad for directions to the post office. The lad told him, and Mr. Moody said to the young fellow, "You know, you must come over to the tent where the revival is taking place." "And why should

I do that?" said the lad. "Well, I am going to preach there." "But still, why would I come?" "Well," said Mr. Moody, "I will show you the way to heaven."

Then the young lad said to him, "You going to show me the way to heaven? You don't know the way to the post office."

✢

Two crofters, as they called farmers in Scotland, were sitting in a Highland church listening to the preacher. He preached an hour . . . an hour and 15 minutes . . . an hour and 20 minutes. Finally, one farmer said to the other farmer, "When is he going to finish?" The other farmer said, "He is finished now. He just won't quit."

✢

At a meeting in one of the cities of the country, a man was elaborately introduced by another man. When the speaker got up and spoke, oh, five or six minutes, a man in the audience, who was from a western city, whipped out a revolver. "What is the matter?" said the speaker. "Did I say something that offended you?" "No," said the man with the revolver. "I am looking for the man who introduced you."

Someone said that some congregations are in the situation of believing that the epistles are wives of the apostles.

Winston Churchill had a reputation for not only being a great statesman but a great elbow-bender in the evenings. At dinner, a woman sitting next to him said, "Mr. Churchill, I think you are drunk." To which Churchill replied, "Yes madam, I am. Tomorrow, I will be sober, but you will still be ugly."

☦

Reverend Wyatt Walker told of a man who was seen crying convulsively. "What's wrong, brother?" I asked.

"My dog died," he said between the sobs.

"You don't have to be bent out of shape over that. You can get another dog."

He stopped crying for a moment and said to me rather gruffly, "I don't want another dog. Roscoe was my friend. He brought me my newspaper and slippers in the evening. He slept with me and I miss him. Sir, are you the preacher here?"

I told him that I was.

"Would you do the funeral?" he quickly asked.

"I don't do dog funerals," I answered rather hurriedly.

"How can I have the funeral?"

I told him, "There is a little church just around the corner from the mosque. Maybe a preacher there can help you." He went on down the street still crying hard.

About a week later I saw him again. He was whistling. There was pep in his step. He got near me.

I said, "How did the funeral go?"

He responded, "Oh, Reverend. It was so beautiful. The lady who sang 'Precious Lord' was out of sight. I gave the preacher $300."

I snorted. "Damn, why didn't you tell me Roscoe was a saved Christian dog?" And the man continued on down the street whistling with pep in his step.

☩

A preacher preached fervently upon the joys of heaven and our desire to go there. After the service, he asked the congregation, "All of you who want to go to heaven, would you stand up?" One man did not stand up. The preacher said, "Son, don't you want to go to heaven?" "Yes sir," he answered the man. "But you sounded like you wanted to carry a bus load out tonight, and I don't want to go then."

☩

In New York, there was at Madison Square Garden a Friday night boxing card. Two boxers were appearing on it. One in the first round used short jabs. There was a sore place and wound showing under his opponent's eye. The man in the other corner started hitting a little harder and closing one eye of the boxer. When he went back to the corner, his second said, "He never touched you, champ." So the boxer turned around and said, "You say he didn't touch me? Then watch the referee. Somebody in there is beating my brains out."

⁜

A man fell out of a 20-story building. As he was falling, a man leaned out of the tenth-floor window and said, "You all right?" The man falling said, "All right so far."

⁜

Two men were arguing. One said to the other, "You are the biggest fool I've ever seen." The other one answered, "Have you ever looked in the mirror?"

⁜

A little boy's mother gave him two apples: one a large, delicious apple and the other a cooking apple, and she said to him, "One is for your little playmate, now give him a choice." Meeting his little friend, obediently he held out the two apples, and said as his mother had told him, "Take your choice." His friend took the delicious apple. The boy with the apples told him, "Put that apple back—and take your choice!"

⁂

My friend Vernon Jordan is one of the managing directors of this international packing firm, and has spent a long time with aging international lawyers. He told me that his wife was carrying him the next night to the opening of the season for the Metropolitan Opera because she, Mrs. Jordan, is one of the board of directors, or one of the moving figures behind the Metropolitan. And so, I told Mr. Jordan of something that a Civil War figure, a prominent lawyer, said. He was escorting his daughter to the Metropolitan Opera. He knew nothing about opera, so he said to her before they went, "Tell me the libretto. Tell me the libretto so I will know how to dilate with the right emotion."

⁂

I knew a public figure in my youth of whom it was said, he was too smart to be called an idiot and too stupid to be called sane.

✢

A man at breakfast was waiting for his wife to prepare some biscuits. He said, "I don't want any biscuits." So, the next day, she prepared some pancakes. "I don't want pancakes." So, the next day, she made some rolls. He said, "I don't want any biscuits. I don't want any pancakes. I don't want any rolls. I want to fuss!"

✢

A man I knew when I was a young man in Louisiana, whose last name was Harris (I forget his first name), was not of a handsome visage. And my uncle used to tell the story; I think it was a joke that Mr. Harris and a bear were fighting. Someone seeing it said, "Come quickly. Something has got a bear."

✢

Laughter Is Good for the Soul

The story is told about President Roosevelt that he had praised a South American dictator as our good friend. One of his cabinet members said, "Mr. President, I hate to tell you this, but this man you praise is . . . I hardly know what to call him. Well, he is really an SOB," to which Mr. Roosevelt is supposed to have replied, "Yes, I know, but he is *our* SOB."

⁂

My mother was a very proper and carefully spoken lady, and she would never say, "It's a hell of a mess." She would say, "This is a mell of a hess."

My father used to tell of a man of some wealth who decided to have the finest steamboat on the Mississippi River, but he also wanted the finest steam whistle ever used by a boat on the Mississippi. The trouble was that when the boat was finished, when the whistle blew there was not enough steam left to move the boat, and when the boat moved there was not enough steam to blow the whistle.

Two women were talking, and one of them said to the other about a third person, "I know that you know what she has told you, but tell me. I'm told she swore you to secrecy, but you can tell me. I can keep a secret." And the first lady said, "I can, too," and did not tell her.

☦

It was a Roman Catholic commentator who said once if the Protestant Church is ever found dead, it will be discovered that it was the sermon that killed it.

☦

My late colleague of 35 years in Brooklyn, Dr. Sandy Ray, was driving through rural Georgia and stopped for gasoline. It was drizzling rain. The attendant came out. Dr. Ray said to him, "Where am I? Where is this?" And the attendant said, "What is the matter, boy? You lost?" "Oh no," Dr. Ray said. "I have a map and I am on the right road; I just don't know where I am right now."

☦

Laughter Is Good for the Soul

Dr. Tom Garrett Benjamin of Indianapolis called me on the telephone, and he was talking about these prosperity preachers and the people who listen to them. People listen to them eagerly. "You can tell their caliber if you will take from the word *masses* that 'm,' and we will find out what the masses can sometimes be."

⁜

In an earlier time, a man was riding in a wagon and being taken to be hanged. People were rushing toward the scene of the hanging several blocks away, rushing, rushing. Finally, the condemned man said, "Don't rush. They can't do anything until I get there."

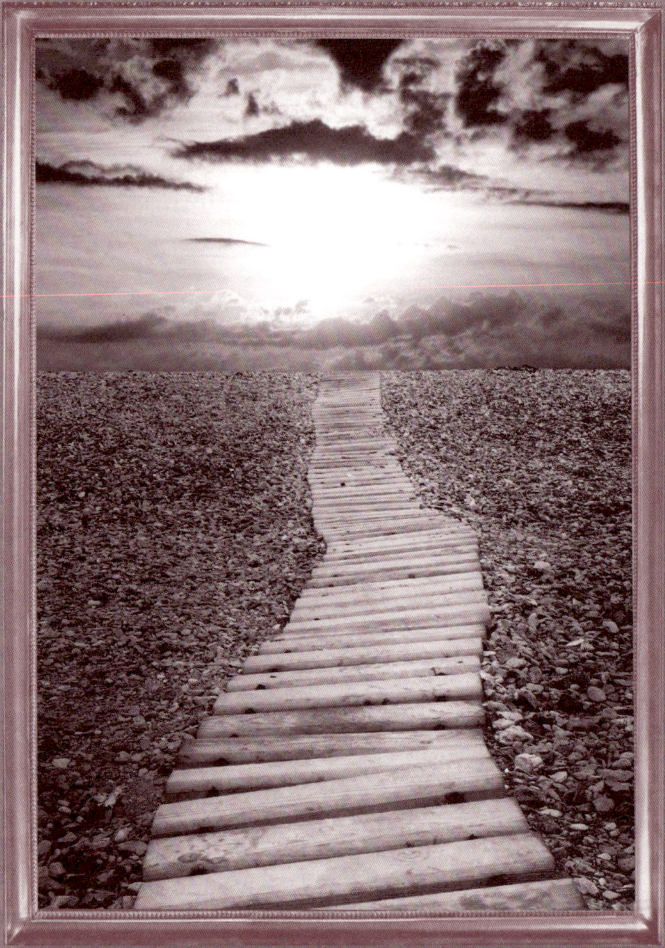

CHAPTER TWELVE

LIFE'S JOURNEY

*L*ife is a bazaar, a county fair with booths and stalls, and life is a midway down which we walk. The lights blaze; the hucksters shout their wares; the music plays. The wise and foolish must pass the booths with their shining articles, their flashing prizes, their tinseled favors, and their eye-catching gifts.

✣

Are the goods worth the cost? How much are we spending? Life is like that. We must ask ourselves questions about our purpose. Are we living in a meaningful way? Are we doing things about which we will be proud? Are we going to find ourselves at an end to the fair, booths closed, and goods gone? We must be careful not to give ourselves for things, which can end up pretty, sad, and tragic.

FAITH IN THE FIRE

Life is not and should not be static. There is activity always going on. We live in a time of creating, shaping, directing movement that is being performed for us. A change is taking place. We laugh sometimes, we cry, we live life, knowing that we are a part of the flow of human existence. Our forbearers recognized the impermanence of life, the transience of health and strength, and that all things of our lives come from a source beyond us. We do not decide on the conditions to which we are born. But, with determination and force, we will take on the challenges with amazing success.

✣

Within us and raging around us, endless conflict exists. We would like to have peace and calm with all of the issues of our lives flowing calmly and peacefully. However, the issues of our lives and the world produce a drama called "the slice of life." The slice produces the conflict and clash, which results in a struggle to develop us into who we will become.

Life's Journey

Life has a precious sound. The word sounds like hope and springtime. It summons an awareness of warmth and laughter and tasks to be eagerly faced and trials to be victoriously met. We struggle against the evils of this world. We struggle against the trials and tribulations of life, drugs, alcohol, poor parenting, bad neighborhoods, and terrible environments. No matter how universal these conditions, we stand on the edge of the yet-to-be. Our best selves are in process. We are running life's race and are determined to cross the finish line despite the obstacles.

※

The great life means walking on a path that leads to radiant and triumphant living. This cannot be measured in the abundance of things which a person possesses. Nor can it be achieved by serving one's self. Triumphant life means dedicating oneself to the goal of serving others.

※

FAITH IN THE FIRE

What a futile life must anyone have who faces all of the uncertainties and imponderables of life with no resources of faith and vision of things unseen. Seeing the disappointments and the cloudy judgments with which we must proceed in so much of life, the physical dangers, and psychic risk we must all take, it must seem often too many; that we cannot bring life off with any honor or decency because we must fight against great obstacles.

Anticipation of great things yet to be is a thoroughly legitimate attitude. This attitude does not necessarily depend entirely on what has already happened. Faith has the power to give substance to things that have not yet come to pass, to clothe hope with reality and to put sinews and flesh on dreams.

Life's Journey

So many of us spend our time looking back to the past as if all the wonderful things that could ever happen have already taken place. Things used to be wonderful for us, but that is past. Of course, we should find strength in the past, but not to live in it as if we have nothing but memories left to us. The past ought to get us ready for the present and the future. The past is of meaning supremely because it gives us hints and clues for the future, not because it affords us luxury of memories out of which the element of uncertainty has been drained. A wise observer has rightly said that the past ought to be a milestone to help us measure the distance we have come; it ought never to be a millstone holding back the adventures that are yet to be.

✣

Read any biography, and if the author has told the truth, he or she will be saying of that life, no matter how noble, no matter how praiseworthy it might be, "We see not all things conquered by that person." Look on any human career from the simplest to the most splendid, and if you can gaze clearly into the heights and depths of that life, see the faults and flaws, the unmastered temptations and the grim failures. We are all subject to failure.

I heard my father long ago preach a sermon on "The Riddle of Life." What is life all about? You will misread it if you decide that life is a picnic, a frolic, or party. Life is a struggle; that is what it is, a struggle from the day we are born until the day we die. Children are barely born, and right where life begins there is a struggle between life and death. You and I will never understand what this life is all about until we see it as a struggle.

✢

We have all faced this in situations. Situations so grim that we did not know whether or not we were going to make it. In those bleak and harsh moments, we face thoughts about what is most important to us. We recall the most cherished of memories, the fellowship found in friends, the care of loving families, and the dangerous paths, which the future may hold. Like the biblical character Job, we are faced with a choice. We may give up and end, or we may believe that though we face a trying hour, we have yet to become all that we are meant to be.

Life's Journey

Forget about the past, if you think it has been the scene of the greatest events that no longer come to pass. Forget the former things, if you think that the days, which are past, have been worn, lost their originality, and are bankrupt in creativity. A new thing can happen. Our job is to cultivate openness and expectancy, wonderful results that can come when a soul preserves openness and readiness.

We ought not to minimize what we face in life. Few situations in life are as bad as we make them, as frightening as we report them. A faulty outward look in your life will produce failure. If you believe that what you are up against in life is too much for you to meet and match and master, even with God's help, then you are already defeated. God gives us a little talent, or much, and a few years and some obstacles, and tells us to make a life.

We talk about wanting to live, we are talking about wanting to see fulfillment that life has a meaning that we believe it was intended to have. We have now begun to suspect that while these tools are wonderful things, they are not exactly the same thing as life. They may augment it, they may supplement it, they may enhance it, but they are not life. The grandest heresy of Western civilization was that life can be lived from the outside inwardly.

✣

We should understand that life couldn't be lived from the outside inwards. You cannot show people on television what America calls the good life, deny them the means to it, and believe that they are going to be satisfied. Life does not consist in the abundance of things. Life cannot be lived from the outside in. Out of the heart are the issues of life.

Life's Journey

Destiny is making itself known to us. There is a language of grace, which we have only learned to stutter in its simplest words. There are vistas and distances that we have not begun to reach. We are growing. A wise person said, "The brook becomes a stream, the stream a river, the river widens to the sea. The infant grows into a child, the child into a youth, the youth into a man." We are becoming and we are not yet what we shall be!

The years have come and gone to sleep wrapped in the shrouds of the past. Is there a person with soul so dense, with heart so cold, that he or she knows not a strange and solemn sense of hush and awe, almost fear, when one realizes that another year is gone? How short seems the time since we gathered between sheltering and beloved walls to see a new season of life come? How quickly the days and months have slipped by bringing with them so many varying experiences and joy and sorrow. What we have done or have not done remains fixed and unalterable. And so, time is gone. We stand a little sad knowing its passage marks the end of a span of opportunity.

⁂

I have always believed that there is some moment in the evening, which resembles as a twin a certain time in the morning. There is a time in the evening of our years when there seems to be momentarily the same quality and quantity as one knew in the morning of life.

⁂

Like dusty travelers on a long and strange journey, we stand at a sharp bend in the road. Behind us we behold the road over which we have come and can never travel again, on before an untrod way, its joys unknown, its sorrows and dangers hidden from view. Looking ahead, we cannot help wondering how it will be for us. What are we going forward into? Will the road we travel next stretch out along level ground with here and there a green and pleasant oasis where we can celebrate the joy of living amidst pleasant company? Will the road wind upward through fierce mountain crags where the snows chill the soul and seldom are encouraging words heard? We do not know.

☩

About the whole voyage of life the question may be, what are you doing here? We reflect that we are like birds, which fly in from a dark night, enter the lighted room of life, flutter around a while in the light, and then suddenly fly out through another door into the mysterious darkness of death. Scriptures speak in a different tone of our transience and impermanence in this life. Some of our elders are no longer among us, but we are in the vigor of life and the sun shines brightly on our pathway as we walk with firm and eager stride toward our destiny.

☩

Some have suggested that our point here is to live a long life. Almost all cultures put great store by the length of life. And yet, somehow we reckon that while age is honorable, life is a more serious transaction than mere length. While long life is greatly to be cherished, this is not why we are here, for the fairest, dearest, loveliest of lives of many of the world's greatest heroes have been those whose lives have been of short duration.

⁕

I ask you, as we stand between an already dead and withering past and an unknown and perilous future, how do you look back on what has gone before and how do you find courage to face whatever is ahead? As I ask you, so I ask myself. Is it well with your soul? The answer should be, yes! We are blessed to be pilgrims on life's journey. I think we sometimes missed the opportunity in this land to be a pilgrim, covenant people. Especially those who have faced great suffering, how they longed to buy some property, educate their children, be somebody, contend for a full share of the American Future.

⁕

Life's Journey

We may think life's answer is pleasure, but in our soberest moments we know that while pleasure may be the sauce of life, it can never be the meat. We may think the answer is money, until we read of someone who has more than his or her share of it committing suicide or making such a mess of his life that we are driven to pity him, though heaven knows we have far less of this world's goods than he. The ultimate, unassailable answer to life is God, not philosophy, since no philosophy can contain the welter and variety of human experience.

The sense of God helps us not to think more highly of ourselves than we ought to, for in awareness of Him as source of life we become sensitive to our "creatureliness"; to the fact that we are neither source nor center of life. The tendency to think more highly of ourselves than we ought robs us of the unutterable joy of thankfulness, since our gratitude for the bounties of life is diminished by our belief that we merit whatever good things have happened to us.

✣

If this kind of dedication could happen, we would thank God for whatever it is in our lives that has driven us to our knees and to our senses. We need to face something too big for us to handle in order to learn how to be humble and pray. I learned how to pray when the old Concord church building burned down. I had been preaching for nearly 15 years, but when I looked on the future of a great church in the balance and my own ministry tested and tried, I learned to pray, to talk to God. I talked with the Eternal like a natural man and asked that our hands be held, that doors would be open for us, to go before us a leading light and on behind us a strong, protecting angel, to not let us get tired or weary. I learned to pray when circumstance knocked me to my knees.

✣

"If my people who are called by my Name, will humble themselves and pray, and seek my face and turn from their wicked ways," that's what we need to do. If there is trouble with your children, humble yourself, pray, seek God's face, in your family life, humble yourself, pray, seek God's face, repent. We are told that we will hear from heaven. Our prayers are heard and our groans and your sighs are understood. God promises to heal us. God will bring back the cooling, life-giving waters. God will heal our land, make it all right, and fix things the way they ought to be. In the darkness, God will make God's light to shine on us; will do for us what we cannot do for ourselves, to fit us for our journey, to undergird us with power from above.

✢

A famous sermon begins, "When life tumbles in, what then." When life does tumble in, at that point or some other point, countless people must make their decision as to what they will do, how they will carry it off when the pilgrimage of life moves from an even path to a rocky road beneath leaden skies and amidst gloomy surroundings. For all of us, life does tumble in over and over again. Life is filled with these interludes of disappointment and sorrow. There are times in life when the days seem hardly worth living, when the sun has left the sky, and we walk through a grim, gray, cloudy time. But, amidst this restless, rolling, raging sea we call life, there is a North Star, a fixed point in creation, a constant in the presence of change, an abidingness where all else is does not matter. Life can be radiant with hope.

We are all pilgrims on the road of life who have taken on the journey. We travel toward life's home. The road of our lives curves by loneliness and dips through the valley of sorrow, the dark glen of betrayal and towns of doubt, but stay on the road. Life can be beautiful with all its succeeding stages and ages a glory, for we are strangers and pilgrims in the earth. Those who are on the journey will get home.

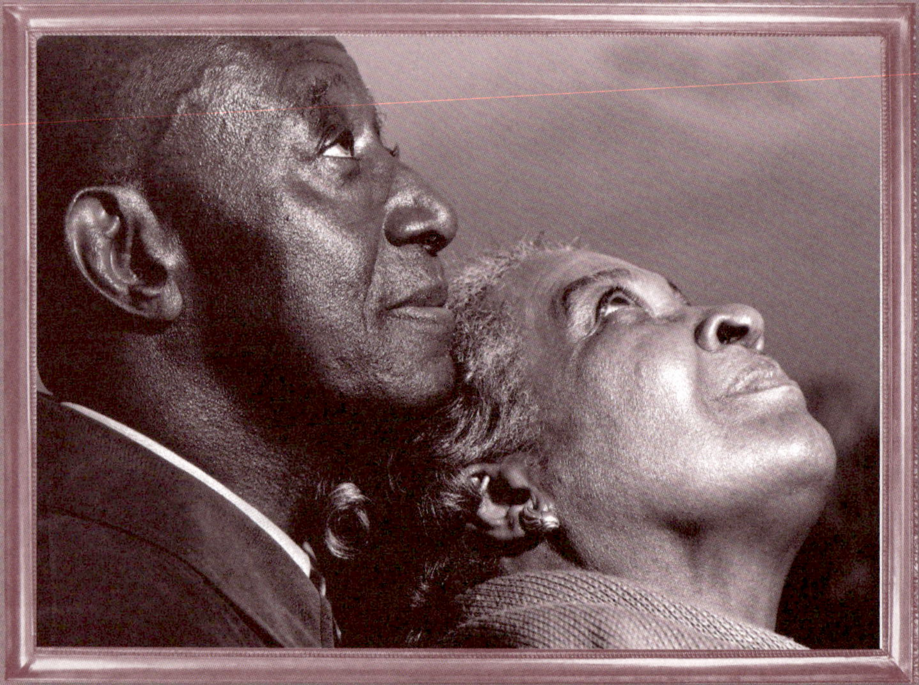

CHAPTER THIRTEEN

THE SWEETENING OF LIFE

"*By* faith, Jacob, when he was a dying, blessed both the Sons of Joseph; and worshipped, leaning upon his staff." (Hebrews 11:21)

☦

Today, I want to turn to consideration of how faith sweetens life. Now, I deliberately chose the term "The Sweetening of Life" in order to draw some initial objection and repudiation in the minds of many of you. I am not unmindful of the fact that "sweetness" is not one of the favorite words of our generation. We look with suspicion upon what is soft, sentimental, and syrupy. All that "sticky jazz," I think the young people call it. I would only plead that what I am talking about in "Sweetening of Life" is not something mushy, teary, sticky, sentimental; not lavender and old lace, but a mellowing and ripening and gladdening of life, which I believe to be for true destiny under God. In other words, I believe that as we grow older, life ought to be sweeter and gentler and mellower. I devoutly believe that faith in Jesus Christ can and will do that in us and for us, to the honor of God's Great Name and to the fulfillment of what our years here are meant to be.

All of us are engaged in the business of growing older. This is as true of the tiniest toddler as it is of the most venerable and aged soul. All too often we grow bitterer as life goes along, and especially in our day and generation. I do not join that chorus of those crying and longing for the good old days, for there was much that was harsh and unlovely about living 25 or 30 years ago. At the same time, I think it an inescapable conclusion that life today is not as leisurely as it once was, though we have more time off from work than men have ever known. We move faster than ever before but we are likely to be more time-conscious and harried about fear of being late than ever before. Never did we have so many healing drugs and never have men been as apprehensive about their health as today. One has only to glance at our comic sheets, apt mirrors of our culture, to see the difference between what life is today in this country and what it once was in terms of our outlook and interests. How many of you remember the delight of the simple, brood comedy of the Katzenjammer Kids, Moon Mullins, and the rest, over and against the grim, serialized bloodletting of the "so-called" comic strips currently popular? Aging has become more tense, less welcome, more grim, tight-lipped, snarling, grasping, ugly, and bitter and selfish.

The Hebrew-Christian religion says that life does not have to grow more bitter and angry as we grow older; it can grow sweeter, mellower, by faith. So of Jacob, the writer of Hebrews says that "By faith, Jacob, when he was a dying, blessed both the Sons of Joseph; and worshipped, leaning upon his staff."

Here Jacob was in a strange land, fated to spend his last days in the land of Egypt, so far from Canaan. A famine had arisen in Canaan and Jacob had been forced to send his children to a strange land in quest of food, for he had heard that there was corn in Egypt. There, in one of the most fascinating narratives in the Old Testament, the Sons came upon Joseph, their brother, whom they had out of envy sold into slavery, now established as an official in Egypt, in charge of food rationing for the nation. One of the heartrending scenes of the Scriptures is enacted as Joseph at last reveals his identity to his terror-stricken brothers, who recognize that this man of great authority is the brother they wronged so long ago. I find it difficult to check the tears when I read how Joseph, unable to restrain himself longer, dismisses his whole staff until only he and his brothers are together. Great sobs convulse his body as he cries out the question about Jacob, "Does my father still live?" I want to preach on that text some day. Then he says to his brothers in a magnificent act of forgiveness, "Be not grieved, it was not you that sent me hither, to Egypt, but God. Bring my father here."

And so Jacob spends his last days with his family in a strange land. He knows that the future of Egypt is fraught with peril. Many trials must come upon his grandchildren. But Jacob has faith in the God of his fathers. As old age comes on, and his steps decline as his vision dims, Jacob is not snarling and fighting and angry and snapping. Faith in God has sweetened the old sharp cynic. The text says as he neared the cold sullen stream of death, there was a sweetness in him born of confidence about the future, "By faith, Jacob when he was a dying blessed both the Sons of Joseph."

The Sweetening of Life

We need faith in the future in order for life to be sweet as we grow older. Not just faith in our personal future, but faith in the future of our family, faith in the future of our church, faith in the future of our race, faith in the future of the church. We are called upon to so work and to so live that the future will be a little better. Boys and girls grown to men and women will rise to call us blessed, if we make our commitment in faith to the future. There is nothing but pointlessness and futility, if all we are spending is on our own bodies and our own appetites. We are then investing only in a grave and a corpse, for this is our physical destiny. We put too much emphasis on the body anyhow, like our marching around at funerals to see the old crumbled shack in which our souls have dwelt and from which they have flown away.

He who invests in the future of God's program sweetens his life. People will rise to call him blessed. I knew in my childhood an ex-slave named Ike Johnson. He took to me when I was a boy. He had never had a chance to go to school, but he always encouraged me to go on to school. "Be somebody," he would say. He would give me a dollar or two when I was in college and say, "Be somebody." I might have made it thus far anyhow, but I call old Ike

Johnson's name in gratitude because he helped me by believing in my future. He sleeps death's long sleep in an unmarked grave in the swamp country of my long ago. At his funeral, a preacher who knew Ike Johnson's interest in me and who is now gone, too, read poetry by Will Dromgoole:

> An old man traveling a lone highway
> Came at the evening cold and gray
> To a chasm vast and deep and wide
> Through which was flowing a sullen tide.
>
> The old man crossed in the twilight dim
> The sullen stream held no fears for him;
> But he turned when safe on the other side,
> And builded a bridge to span the tide.
>
> "Old man" cried a fellow pilgrim near,
> "You're wasting your time in building here
> Your journey will end with the closing day

The Sweetening of Life

You never again will pass this way.
You have crossed the chasm deep and wide,
Why build you this bridge at eventide?"

The builder lifted his old gray head:
"Good friend, in the path I have come," he said
"There followeth after me today

A youth whose feet must pass this way
This stream which has been as naught to me,
To that fair-headed youth may a pitfall be.

He, too, must cross in the twilight dim,
Good friend, I am building this bridge for him."

Only faith in God will give us confidence about the future. We are told repeatedly that mankind holds in his thermonuclear weapons the power to wipe out the world. The Bible does speak of "The heavens disappearing with a loud noise, the elements melting with fervent heat, the earth burned up," but in the same breath the writer of II Peter says that God's vision for the world is not to be frustrated or foiled. He goes on to say, "Nevertheless, we, according to His promise, look for new heavens and a new earth, wherein dwelleth righteousness."

☩

I believe that the future is as bright as God's promises. Great sorrow may pass through the earth; we may in our lifetime see vast giants of military might locked in death struggle. But God's plans are not to be defeated. He has chosen this earth as a fit stage upon which to enact the gallant epic of humanity. That purpose will not fail. God's purpose is going to triumph, "The Kingdoms of this world are going to become the Kingdom of Our Lord and of His Christ. It does not yet appear what we shall be like, but we shall be like Him when He shall appear, for we shall see Him as He is."

☩

Then, at last, this mellowed old man leaned on his staff and worshipped God. What a bright and blessed end. Life had not always been pleasant and sweet for Jacob. There was the bleak hour when vaulting ambition led Jacob to overreach himself and to deceive his father. He must have remembered the disappointment of his father and the anger of his brother all of his life. He has learned that a lot he thought important does not matter, and now, by faith, as old age brings him near his grave, he leans upon his staff and worships God.

This is the same Jacob who, fleet-of-foot, escaped his brother's wrath as a young man and went to live by his wits in a distant land. He had been smart then, even slick, but the years had taught him to put his faith in God. And now, old and weak, leaning on his staff, Jacob worshipped God. Thinking back over his life he had allowed himself to be fooled more than once by his own cunning and bargaining skill, but the years had taught him that lusty ambitions, breathless pushing, roughly elbowing others out of the way all matter very little. Life has something nobler than ambition to offer, dearer than rubies and diamonds, stronger than guns and swords. It is the mercy of God, sometimes sheathed in sunlight, and we call them "joys"; sometimes blessings are clothed in the dark apparel of midnight and we call them "troubles," but all blessings from God's own hand. God leads us along. Realizing that, Jacob, old and weak, leaned upon his staff and worshipped God. The old strength of youth is gone, but by faith the new strength of Grace comes to full power and so Jacob leans on his staff and worships God.

His worship must have struck that note which all true worship must strike. He must have thanked God. Faith will sweeten life for it will make us thankful for all that has happened. For every encouragement anyone has whispered, "Thank God." For every help we receive, "Thank God." For every kind word, "Thanks be to God." For every cruel deed, "Thank God." For every betrayal, "Thanks be to God."

Faith in God can sweeten life. In my childhood I used to hear the old people "tell their determination." Invariably they would say, "Let my last days be my best." Yes, God promises it. "As thy days so shall thy strength be." The road is growing brighter for every believer. Faith says when weakness comes, God will be our strength, and we, leaning on our staff, shall praise our Lord who has brought us all the way. When our footsteps are weary and slowed, faith in Christ Jesus shall make us in Spirit to mount up with wings as eagles; and to run and not be weary and to walk and not faint. When the sun goes down on our heads, and our frames are infirm with age, He will bless us still, and leaning on our staff we can worship God. When our eyes are dim and our vision vague, faith in Christ Jesus will throw visions of rapture upon our gaze. We, leaning on our staff, shall worship God. And in death's high hour from Mount Pisgah's lofty height, we view our home and take our flight. This robe of flesh I'll drop and rise to seize the everlasting prize. And shout while passing through the air, "Farewell."

✢ ✢ ✢

Time & Life Pictures/Getty Images. Photographer Ted Thai

CHAPTER FOURTEEN

FAITH IN THE FIRE

*N*o person is an unbeliever. Every person has faith. A person may not believe in the God in whom I believe. Without faith life would be unbearable because belief has died. We believe in something. The words of the Scripture are true: "Without faith it is impossible to please God."

✜

Faith is not a blind and careless assent to matters of indifference; faith is not a state of mental suspense with hope things may turn out to be as the Bible says. Faith is the firm persuasion that these things are so, and the person who at once knows the magnitude of these things and believes that they are so must be filled with a joy that makes him or her independent of the world, with an enthusiasm which must seem to the world like insanity.

FAITH IN THE FIRE

The chief desire of faith is to know the ways of the One above. We yearn to be able to discern the directions in which we are to move. Growing in faith means coming to understand better and better the paths to which faith will take us. It takes faith, rooted and radiant, to hold on and to hold out, sure that what faith does with us. Everything faith does is to ensure that our peace and joy might be even more complete and that our eyes are fixed evermore on faith.

☦

Faith, from where does it come? Who starts it? Can a person, by searching, find out God? Faith does not start with us. We are not its makers for we are mad. George Buttrick, the gifted preacher from Madison Avenue Presbyterian Church, has put it in a shining phrase, "Faith is not our creation, for we our selves are creatures." Faith comes from beyond us.

☦

It takes some humility to transfer faith from us to God. There is too much stubborn pride in too many of us, and a lot of that pride comes from dumbness and self-deception. We fool ourselves into believing we are better than we are. If sometimes we would face the facts of what we are and what we have been, we would be more humble. Our faith must be transformed from our own shoulders to God.

We hope that God will speak to our faith. When our faith is at its summit, in the confidence that God abides to give meaning and merit to our days, and because God lives, we shall live also. Then every day let us live in that faith until the evening comes and the busy world is hushed and our work is done.

The question may be asked, "Where is your faith?" Faith—not foolish optimism, but faith in the living God. Faith opened it and lo, there was no one there. Faith drives fear forth for it rests our case in God's hands. A worthy faith builds on a sure foundation. It rests on the faith that God is in charge of things.

Faith says we must trust ourselves in His hands. Faith is leaning on God's promises, trusting what God has said, believing that all God has is on the side of love and goodness and righteousness. Faith is a living adventure with God.

☩

Can we be sure about faith, sure enough to act on it? Faith is not the kind of knowledge we crave. What we would like to have and label as faith is a closed-book, proven-set certainty, like two and two equals four. If we knew everything, had seen everything, we knew nothing else was left for us to grasp, we would be fit subjects for a coffin. Sometimes we wish, at least I do, that God had given proof and incontrovertible evidence to all my questions. I submit if He had, life would have no cutting edge, the romance of living would be gone. Life would be reduced to an automatic, robot-like mechanism. Suppose you knew to the hour, the minute everything that was going to ever happen to you, you would be as bored with living as having to sit through a movie for a second time when you know that whole plot and denouement. The days would be as dull.

As in the case of Abraham, we learn that it takes faith to deal with God. Abraham is called the father of the faithful. Abraham is a man whom God promises blessings: to be father of a great nation in a new land even when he is old and childless. Yet, he left his native land in pursuit of the promises made to him. Abraham's very footsteps toward a new land became to deed the land that has been promised. By faith, Abraham received the promises of God. We must believe by faith that the promises will come to pass! It takes faith to believe when the promises are huge and sometimes seem long-delayed. We must learn to wait on "faith-work." We must think, pray, try, and wait on faith!

One of the greatest figures of history we could imitate is Abraham. He acted in faith. One must recognize that this man's faith has made him faithful, and that the noblest commentary on human life is his epitaph, by faith. By faith he tarried in the land of promise, though it seemed a strange country. By faith he dwelt in tents with Isaac and Jacob, who through him became joint heir of the same promise. By faith he looked for a city, which hath foundations whose builder, and maker, is God. By faith, he and Sarah's children became a multitude, a number, like the stars of the sky, and as the sand, which is by the seashore, innumerable.

Faith does not work in a vacuum. We live in the promises of life and only those who live in the climate of faith appropriate those promises. The faithful have not lived as if they have already tasted doubt. We need not be anxious because we have confidence in a strong and abiding faith.

☩

There are those people who try to remove faith from the actualities of life. Here on Earth, our faith worked out. Faith ought ever to reprove them and to bring them to the awareness, that in the midst of our mud, dirt, glory, and grandeur, our faith was worked out. This faith will never mean anything until it means something in the actual context of our daily problems. This is what faith is all about, and to separate it from that is to separate it from its source and from its sustenance. It is a leap of faith beyond the power of reason to explain, but we discover in our walk the reason that at least confirms what faith declares—our belief in God. That is the final mystery of faith.

We have come this far by faith. Nobody lives without it. Faith has brought us thus far. Such faith is built upon our experience. Faith must have a heritage. We all take inspiration and strength of spirit from the example of those who have stood fast in the faith. Faith does not spring full-blown and grown; it must have roots. Those roots must sink in the ground of experience. People's faith easily changes when it is not rooted and grounded. But, deep and radical experiences confirm our faith. We can go back to the scenes and places, to situations and circumstances, and realize it was our faith that saw us through. We have come this far not by wealth or earthly goods. We have come this far by faith.

Faith changes a person and one man's faith can change other people's lives. The faith we now practice has come to most of us because there was an example in the homes of our childhood of devotion and love of God. Granted, that sooner or later we must test in the sometimes-hard and sometimes-softly-treacherous places of our own experience the faith which is ours. Many of us have been saved from awful and terrible things because we were held by the invisible hands of giant memories of praying fathers and devout mothers.

Still the first glimmer of it comes from those who, by fireside and at dinner table, repeat in tender love the faith that can be ours.

✧

Sometimes it may be discouraging if you are in a family where it is difficult or awkward to profess your faith. A long time your faith may not be embraced by others, but after a while that steady influence, that bright and sunny disposition, that faithfulness, that light of faith in your eye, that calmness in the midst of criticism, that peacefulness will have its effect.

✧

The faith of the fireside follows us all through life. Some of us never come to a hard place without remembering a certain word so often on the lips of those from a previous generation. Faith may seem to disappear after great tribulation and the passing of many years. But, in the hour of need, sorrow, or a calm memory, a wisp of half-forgotten faith will return like fond benedictions. The faith from home follows us!

✣

We are all held by the faith that it can be better for us. This is not fanciful wishing; this is a gift of God. Some faith in a better day may be, as Patrick Henry said, "the fond illusions of hope," but we live upon the lively hopes that we have. Every person ought to be straining to catch sight, some glimpse of the better that can be in him.

As a people of faith, be faithful.
This matter of faithfulness is not small or cheap advice. It does not mean slavishness. There is about faithfulness a nobler quality, a more splendid grandeur than mere regularity. Faithfulness is a quality of God which means true to one's character and to one's calling. Faithfulness is an attribute of God.

In all your doing, hold out and prove yourself faithful. If the road is rough and rocky; if we fall; if our strength fails; if turned around; if unappreciated; don't give up. In all, be people who are called faithful. Such must be the faith of believers. We must be committed even in our struggles to the faith that righteousness will prevail. Your victory will be there for the world to see. Beyond your ken and understanding, your faith will be reasserted. There is a faith, founded in God, in which God will bring to pass what God has begun. It is the faith that no life committed to God can fall beyond God's grasp. In this way, the drama of our faith is unfolded.

☦

Faith is power. It is filled with love. Faith reminds us of who loves us and how deep we are in the heart of the One above. Faith has the power to make those who are lost confident that the One will come looking for us. Faith has the power to make those who have gone into far countries know that their names are remembered. Faith has the power to heal the hurt, to bind up the wounded, to preach deliverance to those who are captive.

✢

We have found our faith in the keeping power of God in flames and trials. Our faith, which holds, is born in the fire. All of us who have won are winning our faith in the fires, which have swept our lives. Those fires that scorch our inmost souls and sear our noblest dreams can declare that we know no other strength but that strength which is from above.

We have won our faith in fire. When the structures of our lives are destroyed by flames, and the hungry flames of life seem to devour that beauty like a starving man before a laden table, we know that we are not alone. Faith still lives! Faith is not burned. Promises are not scorned. Faith guides us, holds us, and sustains us. By faith, the impossible will come to pass. By faith, defeat can be turned into victory and sorrow into laughing. Faith will see you through and make us more than conquerors.

Faith pleases God. Faith gives energy to hope. Faith gives substance to hope. Faith clothes hope with flesh and sinew. Faith puts muscle in expectation. Faith gives substance and body to things hoped for. Faith provides evidence for what is not yet seen. Faith can move mountains. Faith will last when all else is gone.

✣ ✣ ✣

MY FAVORITE THINGS

Favorite Books:

The Bible

Positive Preaching and Modern Mind by Peter Forsyth

A Tale of Two Cities by Charles Dickens

Books by Horatio Alger, Jr.

For We Have This Treasure by Paul Scherer

Gone With the Wind by Margaret Mitchell

Up from Slavery by Booker T. Washington

Walking with God by James Stewart

Jesus Came Preaching by George Arthur Buttrick

W. E. B. Du Bois: Biography of A Race by David Levering Lewis

W. E. B. Du Bois: The Fight for Equality and the American Century, 1919–1963 by David Levering Lewis

Favorite People in World History:

Jesus

The Apostle Paul

Howard Thurman

Samuel DeWitt Proctor

Booker T. Washington

Favorite Speakers:

Nannie Helen Burroughs

Abraham Lincoln

W. E. B. Du Bois

Sandy F. Ray

Winston S. Churchill

Martin Luther King, Jr.

Julius C. Austin

Senator William E. Borah

Washington Monroe Taylor

Marshall Shepard, Sr.

Favorite Plays:

A Streetcar Named Desire by Tennessee Williams

Your Arms Too Short to Box with God, music and lyrics by
   Alex Bradford and a book by Vinnette Carroll, who also directed.

Fences by August Wilson

Favorite Teams:

New Orleans Saints

The Brooklyn Dodgers

Pittsburgh Steelers 1970s

McKinney High School Panthers, Baton Rouge, LA

ACKNOWLEDGMENTS

Dr. Taylor and I appreciate the contributions of those who made *Faith in the Fire* possible. We thank Mrs. Phillis Taylor whose love, care and devotion to Dr. Taylor and his ministry have made all of our lives the richer. We thank LaTrice Taylor for her love and constant review of this manuscript. We are especially grateful for the Reverend Sherri A. Graham who-took responsibility for having material included in "Everyday Wit" and "Laughter is Good for the Soul" recorded and transcribed which made those chapters possible. We appreciate Drs. Reggie High and Jerome Washington for their unique personal care of Dr. Taylor which makes them diamonds among gems. We are most grateful for the Reverend Julie Bell, Esq. for her adroit legal advice and counsel. Furthermore, we will be forever grateful to Tavis Smiley and Cheryl Woodruff for their spirits of love, faith, sincerity, industry and for allowing our vision for this book to become a reality.

ABOUT THE AUTHOR

Dr. Gardner C. Taylor, born in 1918, is a graduate of Leland College and the Oberlin Graduate School of Theology. Named "Dean of African American Preachers" by *Time* magazine, he served the Concord Baptist Church of Brooklyn as its senior pastor for 42 years. Dr. Taylor is the author of several books, including the six-volume series *The Words of Gardner Taylor*. Having had a prolific ministry as a clergyman and advocate for social justice, he and his wife, Phillis, now reside in Raleigh, North Carolina.

ABOUT THE EDITOR

The **Reverend Edward L. Taylor,** a native of Ville Platte, Louisiana, was educated at Louisiana College, New Brunswick Seminary, University of London, and has been a Resident Fellow at Harvard Divinity School. He is the editor of *The Words of Gardner Taylor, The Gardner C. Taylor Preaching Library on CD-Rom,* and the *Essential Taylor Audio Series.* Rev. Taylor and wife, LaTrice, have one son, Paul "Bishop" Taylor. Over the past 14 years, he has served as the pastor of several congregations. He currently resides in San Jose, California; and London, England.

✧ ✧ ✧

We hope you enjoyed this SmileyBooks publication.
If you would like to receive additional information, please contact:

SMILEYBOOKS

Distributed by:
Hay House, Inc.
P.O. Box 5100
Carlsbad, CA 92018-5100
(760) 431-7695 or (800) 654-5126
(760) 431-6948 (fax) or (800) 650-5115 (fax)
www.hayhouse.com® • www.hayfoundation.org

✧ ✧ ✧

Published and distributed in Australia by: Hay House Australia Pty. Ltd. • 18/36 Ralph St.
Alexandria NSW 2015 • ***Phone:*** 612-9669-4299 • ***Fax:*** 612-9669-4144 • www.hayhouse.com.au

Published and distributed in the United Kingdom by: Hay House UK, Ltd. • 292B Kensal Rd.,
London W10 5BE • ***Phone:*** 44-20-8962-1230 • ***Fax:*** 44-20-8962-1239 • www.hayhouse.co.uk

Published and distributed in the Republic of South Africa by: Hay House SA (Pty), Ltd.
P.O. Box 990, Witkoppen 2068 • ***Phone/Fax:*** 27-11-467-8904 • www.hayhouse.co.za

Published and distributed in India by: Hay House Publishers India • Muskaan Complex,
Plot No. 3, B-2, Vasant Kunj, New Delhi 110 070 • ***Phone:*** 91-11-4176-1620
Fax: 91-11-4176-1630 • www.hayhouse.co.in

Distributed in Canada by: Raincoast • 9050 Shaughnessy St., Vancouver, B.C. V6P 6E5
Phone: (604) 323-7100 • ***Fax:*** (604) 323-2600 • www.raincoast.com

✧ ✧ ✧